CHRIS WILD is an author, care home consultant, government advisor, national youth advisor for young people and a charity patron for twenty charities. He is a passionate advocate and campaigner, appearing on the BBC and *Newsnight*.

His first book, *Damaged*, told the story of his life and those of the other young children in care he met along the way. You can find him on Twitter @ccwild79, where he would love to hear from you.

The State of It

Stories from the frontline of
a broken care system

CHRIS WILD

JB

First published in the UK by John Blake Publishing
an imprint of Bonnier Books UK
4th Floor, Victoria House
Bloomsbury Square,
London, WC1B 4DA
England

Owned by Bonnier Books
Sveavägen 56, Stockholm, Sweden

www.facebook.com/johnblakebooks ⊙
twitter.com/jblakebooks ◪

Hardback ISBN: 978-1-789-463-89-7
Paperback ISBN: 978-1-789-463-90-3
eBook ISBN: 978-1-789-463-91-0
Audiobook ISBN: 978-1-789-463-92-7

A CIP catalogue of this book is available from the British Library.

Typeset by Envy Design Ltd
Printed and bound in Great Britain by Clays Ltd, Elcograf S.p.A.

1 3 5 7 9 10 8 6 4 2

For each book sold, Bonnier Books UK shall donate 1% of net receipts across all editions of
The State of It to Become, a charity registered in England and Wales, charity number 1010518.

John Blake Publishing is an imprint of Bonnier Books UK
www.bonnierbooks.co.uk

To anyone who reads this, in a world where you can be anything, be kind and always remember that children in care are still children.

Contents

The State of It

I WAS TAKEN INTO care after the sudden death of my father when I was 11, in 1992. Before that, our family life had been pretty ordinary, just me, Mum, Dad and my sister Donna.

My dad, Dave Cockcroft, was something of a local legend around Boothtown in Halifax where we lived. His dad had vanished as soon as he was born and his mum died when he was a child, so he'd grown up in the care system and was pretty streetwise. But he was also well known for his fairness and generosity. A tough man with a kind heart. Around his family, he rarely spoke about his time living in care homes and with various foster placements. When he did, his words revealed little but his eyes were filled with pain. I remember the first time he mentioned his 'children's home' in front of me. I was maybe eight or nine years old and in my wide-eyed innocence I'd asked what it was, excitedly imagining scenes of fun and adventure, like in *Swallows and Amazons*. But Dad's response was abrupt and resolute.

'It's a place you'll never, ever experience,' he said.

Unfortunately life had a different plan.

Dad caught chickenpox that developed into shingles and

1

that was what killed him, of all things. After his death, Dad's foster brother Viv crept into Mum's life. Widowed and left with two children at the age of 30, she needed someone to lean on but everyone could see he was a vulture. Everyone except poor Mum, that was. Maybe she was so blinded by grief that she didn't notice him circling the scraps of the life that Dad had worked so hard to build.

Somehow, within six months of Dad passing away, he'd moved into our family home, casting a shadow of violence over us all. If Mum so much as looked at him the wrong way or didn't have tea on the table in time he'd beat her black and blue. Then he started on me and Donna too. Once he'd physically broken Mum down, he picked away at her emotionally. He gaslit her and manipulated her for his own ends, even convincing her to sell our family home and move in with him.

Once she was under his roof, the power was all his.

I turned to the streets to escape my crumbling home. At the age of 11, drinking, fighting, taking drugs and stealing became my solace and the streets of Halifax my playground. As much as Dad's name had been renowned around town, so too was mine, but for all the wrong reasons. If something went missing, a window was smashed or a bloody nose was doled out, I usually had something to do with it. I wore my reputation like a badge of honour. But after 12 months and six arrests Mum couldn't cope with my behaviour and a decision was made. I was to be sent to Skircoat Lodge Children's Home.

When it was first suggested, Mum refused, knowing it was

the last thing my dad would have wanted. But by then, Viv was her puppet master and pulled all the strings. Between him and my social worker, she eventually relented.

Given my dad's warning tone about children's homes, I probably should have felt more scared as I approached the unwelcoming heavy doors of Skircoat Lodge and noted the thick glass windows with dents in the frames where people had tried to break in – or out, maybe? But I didn't. I felt excited, not just because I was getting away from Viv, but because it all felt like a big adventure. The tall, broad man who had greeted me and shown me to my room – the Boss Man, as I called him – didn't seem all that scary and I was going to be living away from home, and with a roommate too.

What fun we'd have!

That illusion was quickly shattered when I met Callum. He was 14 years old but had the mental capacity of a 10-year-old and the personal hygiene of a tramp. While I wanted to talk about girls and drinking, all he was interested in was superheroes and comics.

'He's slow,' people told me. 'Not the full ticket.'

I quickly learned that people abused that 'slowness', something I now understand was a serious mental health condition. But they didn't care about things like that back then. He'd do anything for a cigarette and ended up in all kinds of precarious situations in pursuit of his next smoke. At the time, I never questioned what might have made him that way but years later I found out that he'd been sexually abused by his grandfather from the age of eight. At the children's home, his trauma was never dealt with; he was simply left to rot.

Callum was the first broken soul I met on my journey in the sector but not the last.

While I was at Skircoat Lodge, there was Claire, a few years older than me and a goddess in my teenage eyes, but also one of the Boss Man's favourites. On occasion, when I'd been told to take some items to his room, she opened the door in tiny night shorts, behind her a bed strewn with chocolates and – oddly, I'd thought at the time – girlie magazines.

Girls don't read titty magazines, do they?

There was Lottie too, who I got on with well. The Boss Man wasn't so interested in her so she usually got in trouble the same way me and Callum did – a beating here or there. But after we got caught misbehaving one night, the Boss Man's right-hand woman – who we all called the Bear – meted out my punishment while Lottie was simply sent to bed without supper.

I felt every blow from the Bear but I was glad Lottie didn't have to go through it. I thought she'd escaped but she hadn't. After a while she just vanished.

'Sent to a care home in Wales,' the whispers around town said. 'They drugged her so she'd go quietly.'

It didn't take long for me to understand why my dad had never wanted me to end up in a home. It was no adventure and certainly no fun. You took a beating at the drop of a hat, for one thing. Once, I'd been buttering toast in the kitchen when I'd suddenly felt a blow to the side of my head. It was the

Boss Man. My crime? Buttering toast 'the wrong way'. I tried to run away time and again but the police always brought me back and another beating would follow. The more the physical abuse happened, the more I rebelled. God knows what would have happened if I'd stayed. You see, in a strange twist of fate, one night when the police picked me up in town raising more merry hell, they took me back to my grandma and grandad's instead of the home.

'Thank you, officer. He'll do better here with us,' my grandma said.

And that was that. My time in a care institution was over but my journey through the care system wasn't.

I'm not proud to say that I didn't make life easy for my grandparents. I was spinning through life like a rebel without a clue. I befriended a gang from a local estate, the 'Bus Station Crew'. At 13 years old I was hanging out with drug dealers, burglars, addicts and prostitutes, listening to dance music that I needed to take acid to keep up with.

I was an immediate asset. Being a child, my slight frame meant I could squeeze into small windows and jam my arm through letterboxes to loosen flimsy locks. I could break, enter and leave without a trace and I could sprint like a whippet away from police. Without Dad holding us together I was adrift and this band of petty criminals and heroin addicts became my family. I was left to run riot and – despite the fact that I was still a child, a heartbroken, damaged and lost child – the authorities had already washed their hands of me.

I was abandoned by the system.

What followed was a 15-year journey to hell and back. Every step I took led me to another broken soul that revealed more of the truth about the care system I'd escaped. Thanks to a series of saviours, good people who tried their best to help me, I did manage to extract myself from the criminal lifestyle I'd engaged in but the addiction to drink and drugs was harder to shake. I tried time and again to escape the magnetic pull of Halifax and the dark circles I mixed in. I took up boxing and tried to fight my way out. I became an actor and tried to bury my reality in a character of my own making. I went to LA and attempted to start again.

But their stories kept haunting me.

Tales of young girls and boys, some as young as six, being raped repeatedly by their key workers. Teenage girls being plied with chocolates and alcohol and coerced into providing strangers with sexual favours in return for 'privileges' like sweets, TV time and a later curfew. Broken and vulnerable youngsters being shipped from home to home to be used and abused by this network of wolves.

And when they snapped and lashed out or lost their grip on any sense of sanity? Then it was off to a secure unit where they could be locked away and forgotten about forever. They were just sacks of flesh. Those in control knew that no one would care what happened to them.

Over the years, so many of those I'd met in the system – or after they'd left it – moved on from this world. Suicide, overdose and criminal misadventure. Deep down I knew that they'd all met their end because of a system that had chewed them up and spat them out. I could hear their desperate cries and I began to wonder if I would ever escape their voices.

I guess it was a form of survivor's guilt. The wolves had circled me but I'd always been able to stay one step ahead. *Why?*

By the age of 27, I had no real friends, no money and even my family had given up on me. I couldn't take it anymore. I'd failed the people who had tried to help me yet I was still here when others who'd never had such a chance weren't. There were people still in the system, still suffering, and I was just burying my head and trying to escape the knowledge.

I believed that I didn't deserve to be here anymore and decided to make my twenty-eighth birthday my last. I collected my dole money and, instead of scrabbling to pay off my most urgent drug debt, I took a tour of my local pubs, sinking a few pints in each and chatting with friends and acquaintances, then I went back to my mum's old house and let myself inside. I found a length of rope, made a noose based on what I'd seen in the movies and tied it to a solid oak beam in the ceiling. It seemed like the best place to die. Where the violence started and where my life veered off course.

I slugged back neat vodka and snorted fat lines of cocaine until I was calm and ready. I stood on a chair, put the noose around my neck, took a deep breath and went to jump. I leaned forward and the noose tightened, causing my breathing to become erratic and spots to form in front of my eyes.

But I couldn't jump.

It was as if something was pushing against my chest and holding me firmly in place. A mysterious force that I couldn't break through. A hand fighting hard against the momentum of my intended fall. *Dad?*

Suddenly the calmness inside me was shattered; spluttering, I fought to loosen the coils that secured the noose until I collapsed onto the chair, swallowing the air hungrily, gasping in big mouthfuls. At first I felt like a failure. I couldn't even kill myself right. But then I realised, this was rock bottom. This was the place I'd been heading to since the day Dad died. I'd got there.

And I'd survived.

After that, I felt I'd been given another chance to live. A chance that I had to make the most of. I left Halifax and moved to London, fully aware that the town was a part of my painful past, a wound that needed time to heal. I continued to meet people who had been through the care system and seen its horrors. But instead of being sucked into a dark place, I realised they'd survived – and I could too.

None had as big an impact on me as Samantha.

Samantha had been put into care at another children's home that was run by the same council as Skircoat Lodge. Everything she told me was reminiscent of what I'd seen during my time in the home. But in place of the Boss Man and the Bear they had Mr Brown and Miss Black. She described a night to me when Mr Brown invited her into his room and offered her cakes and chocolates and alcohol. As a 13-year-old usually deprived of such treats, she readily accepted. Hours later, she'd woken up in her bed, on a plastic-covered mattress, in a pool of her own blood and with a stabbing pain in her rectum.

She was shattered by her experience, but Samantha was different to some of the other care kids I'd met. Her experience didn't break her spirit. Instead, she channelled her anger and started fighting for justice. Not just for her but for victims of the system everywhere.

'So far we have managed to get 50 of the bastards convicted for rape and sexual abuse and sent to jail,' she told me. 'This is my life now. This is how I moved on.'

I was inspired into action and wondered how I might be able to make a difference like Samantha was. I'd always known things at Skircoat Lodge weren't right when I was there but her story was like a spotlight shining on my life. I did some research and discovered that the home had been closed in 1996 due to a damning report published by the NSPCC in 1994. In 1995, an allegation of rape had been brought against the Boss Man – Malcolm Osric Phillips – and in 1997 an independent investigation was launched by Calderdale Social Services. Called Operation Screen, it ran until 2002 and went right back to the 1980s. In 2001, during the course of the investigation, Phillips was jailed for seven years for 12 counts of indecent assault on a female under 14, one count of indecent assault on a female over 16 and one count of indecency with a girl under 16.

His colleague, Andrew Shalders, was locked up for 15 years for 11 counts of indecent assault on a male under 14, one count of indecent assault on a male under 16 and two counts of indecency with a boy under 16. Another worker, Terence Thomas O'Hagan, was charged with buggery of a male under the age of 16 and indecent assault on a male under 16 but he had died before he was convicted.

It seemed I'd been lucky that they'd left before I was sent to the home.

There were similar investigations into historic child abuse in North Wales. In the run-up to the trials they lost 19 victims to suicide. By that point, I could myself count 22 old friends from the care system who had either killed themselves or died of a drug overdose. I couldn't bring any of them back but I could start making a change now. I owed it to them all.

That was how my professional career in the care sector began. I studied for my NVQ level two in social care and gained the legal qualification that would support my lived experience and passion for working in the sector. It was only then that I realised just how vast and complex the system is. For one, I'd never realised just how late I'd come into the system – or how quickly I'd left it.

I learned about the full cycle that many go through. While there are some children's homes that look after toddlers, ordinarily children start to enter the system around the age of ten. There are a number of options, like adoption or a series of foster placements. If foster placements can't be found, or if they break down, that is when children's homes come into the picture. If you end up in the system between the ages of 10 and 16, you'll either be fostered or – more often than not – placed in a children's home that's run by the local council and regulated by Ofsted.

Children's homes are regulated because they provide what is defined as formal 'care'. This could mean lots of things, from providing a safe place for those who have been subjected to abuse and neglect, to supporting those with physical or mental health conditions. After the age of 16 though, this support ends. Nothing is perfect up to this point, believe me. But it is what happens after that shocked me the most. You see, the waters muddy when it comes to post-16 provisions.

Most young people leave a children's home or foster care and go into semi-independent accommodation. These are predominantly privately run and unregulated because they provide 'support' rather than 'care'. The standard of that support varies widely and the lack of regulation also gives rise to unregistered provisions – houses where young people in the system might end up through lack of guidance or choice. They presume to provide some forms of 'care' without being registered by Ofsted and they rarely give young people anything like the kind of support they need.

Once you reach semi-independent care, you have two years, 24 months, in which to prepare yourself to live independently, before the support available is ripped away from you and you are left without a safety net.

My personal experience meant that I decided to start out working in children's homes – the type regulated by Ofsted that provided care services. I looked after children who were from disadvantaged backgrounds or had been abandoned or abused. I wanted to help kids that were like the people I had known growing up, to try to give them a chance. I taught them boxing and acting as extra-curricular activities and it felt great seeing them grow in confidence and learn new skills.

On the surface the system was nothing like the one I'd left. Everything seemed tighter, cleaner and safer. Regulation meant there were inspections, processes and procedures. But it was a fragile façade. Every staff member I came across had a story to tell about previous homes, as did every new child. It was two sides of the same negative story. Underpaid and stressed-out workers complaining about young people in their care verbally and physically attacking them. Young people in care sharing tales of care workers who neglected their duties in favour of sitting in the office all day, or who beat up and bullied them.

North, south. Private, public – it was all just a big fucking mess.

In the children's home I tried to make changes, testing out new approaches and encouraging the kids to engage in sport and creative therapies. But the old guard in this highly regulated system didn't like change. Many were just riding out their last working days before they could collect a fat pension and saw me as a troublemaker.

When I introduced boxing and fitness lessons, art therapy, creative writing classes and drama sessions, I watched as the kids in the home embraced the things that had saved me and I felt like I'd found my purpose.

While some of my colleagues praised me for being innovative, I continued to run up against the attitude of the old guard.

'What's the point?' they'd say. 'They'll all end up in jail, or on the streets.'

Or dead.

'The point is they deserve a chance. They deserve our attention,' I argued.

But my words fell on deaf ears. Just as in the care homes I had started in, they were often worn down by years of understaffing, long hours and poor pay. They'd felt that they'd done their time. They were also just riding out the last few years until their pension and didn't want a little upstart like me rocking the boat.

Their attitude made me seethe. Rather than dissuade me from making changes, it put even more fire in my belly. I wasn't going to let this generation of kids be let down. I continually stuck my head over the parapet, challenging colleagues' attitudes, fighting for more budget for the activities I knew first-hand had the potential to change and even save lives.

I ignored those who warned me against it.

'You'll slip up, Chris.'

I didn't really know what they meant until it happened. It seemed that people trying to make change were viewed as troublemakers. In the end, it seemed that I'd rocked the boat a little too much with my new ideas and they found a way to let me go.

Losing a job that gave me purpose could have crushed me but instead it propelled me once again into my sanctuaries of art and writing. I put pen to paper and started documenting my own personal story about growing up in the care system in Halifax in the 1980s, alongside the stories of the care home kids I'd met along the way. Some of them had made it out the other side, like me, and some hadn't. I'd carried their stories and their pain for years although I hadn't realised it until the words started pouring out of me. Writing was cathartic and the notes that I scribbled down then became my first book, *Damaged*.

While writing the book, I decided to move into the semi-independent support sector. This is the part of the system that looks after children as they move towards adulthood. After leaving a children's home or perhaps a foster family at 16, the law deems them old enough to fend for themselves and to only need 'support' rather than formal, regulated care services. The houses I went on to manage looked after young people who had reached that point.

Despite that fact that young people from 'normal' backgrounds are considered children until they are 18, the 16- and 17-year-olds in our homes weren't viewed in the same light. They came from places of trauma – broken and abusive homes and corrupt or war-torn countries. They had behavioural needs and mental health issues, yet they were considered too old to be 'in care' and receive the specialist support that children's homes provide.

We were there to bridge the gap. To help them learn how

to live independently after leaving a children's home or foster family, or on arriving in a strange country after a terrifying journey with nothing but the clothes on their back.

The way kids leave children's homes in the UK is fucked. At 16, when most of their peers are studying for GCSEs, going on first dates and sneaking off to the park to drink obscure alcohol smuggled from their parents' spirits cupboard, kids leaving children's homes are having the only support and security they've known most of their lives pulled from underneath them like a rug. They're being ushered towards adulthood whether they're ready or not, with two years – *just two years* – to prepare them for when they are pushed off what we professionals call the 'care cliff' – the point when support ends – at the age of 18.

After that they're left to fend for themselves.

When I'd first started working in these unregulated houses, I'd seen it as an opportunity to balance my own life and to really make a difference to these kids' lives. I wanted to continue to help kids who found themselves in the care system, often through no fault of their own. Kids just like me. Some I'd worked with had lived with alcoholic parents, were survivors of abuse or simply had learning difficulties or mental health problems that their families couldn't manage. They weren't bad kids, as the outside world and sometimes even the staff looking after them seemed to think. They were just lost, neglected, damaged. They needed help to find their way off the road that was leading them towards their own personal disasters. I knew there was hope for these kids, but the help on offer in the system needed shaking up.

And I wanted to be the one to do the shaking.

When my book, *Damaged*, was published, it not only freed the ghosts of my pain, it gave me a platform too.

A place where I could be the upstart again.

A voice for care home kids, past and present.

That's what this book has been for me, too. A chance to be a voice for those who do not have one. To shine a light on the entire care sector. All of the abuses that happen in the system, the neglect, historic sexual abuse, lack of opportunities and inequity, I will try to shed more light on.

They are already documented in court cases, investigations and books, like my first, showing the entire care system is not fit for purpose. But we can't look at the sector in siloes anymore. And we can't ignore what is happening to our most vulnerable children when they become adults in the eyes of the care system. These young adults and older children are racing against a ticking clock, trying to access the life skills they need to survive faster than anyone else – despite starting further back from the finish line, after spending most of their lives in a broken system. If they don't make it to that finish line in time, there is nothing more for them. They are written off, forgotten and abandoned.

The system is in a state. It is broken and it has to change.

By telling you *how* it's broken, I'm going to show you how we might just be able to fix it, too.

CHAPTER ONE
Part of the Problem

I STARTED WORKING IN privately run, unregulated houses specifically for boys over the age of 16 as contract staff in 2017. I had vowed to work with older kids, to try to get to them before they were completely abandoned by the state once they were considered adults. At the same time, I was fighting for justice for victims of historic sexual abuse in children's homes and campaigning for better support for kids in modern care homes. John already knew all about me when I applied for the job managing one of his houses. He ran a small group of houses in the South East that supported young men in the care system. After he interviewed me for the role, it didn't take him long to get back in touch.

It felt like validation after what I'd been through working in council-run children's homes. Here was someone who appreciated my experience, who wasn't afraid to let me try new things and who allowed me to work the way I wanted to work, free from the endless bureaucracy of the public sector.

Before, there had been no time for me to do anything more than what my day job required and I hadn't been allowed to act as a figurehead for the campaigning work that I'd become involved in separately. But in my new role, if I got all my work done in three days, the rest of the time was mine to use as I saw fit.

Campaigning.

Giving extra support to the kids in my care.

Spending time with my family.

I knew I was good at my job, John trusted me implicitly and quickly asked me to manage two more of the houses he owned, with responsibility for eight members of staff. But I wasn't too naïve to realise that my profile had been a factor in my appointment. My first book had catapulted me onto a national stage. I'd become a regular guest on current affairs shows, written opinion pieces for national media and been interviewed for radio stations all over the country, talking about how social care for children needed to change. I had the ear of sector leaders, celebrities and even government ministers who wanted someone with actual lived experience of the sector – personally and professionally – to help them shape the future for children in care in the UK.

John loved the glitz of it all, the kudos. In return for letting him bask in the glow of what he perceived as my 'celebrity', I got better pay than I'd ever had in my life, the flexibility to pick and choose how and when I worked and the opportunity to manage some of his houses as I saw fit. For the first time in years, I felt professionally and personally free. No longer handcuffed by regulators and processes that had made it nearly impossible to make an impact on the kids' lives, everything about how I could interact and engage with the kids changed.

And I loved it.

The only downside to the arrangement – and it was big one – was that I was the first point of call if the shit hit the fan. The houses I worked in seemed to have a seasonal cycle, laying almost dormant in the summer and coming to life in winter, a hive of activity under the cover of darkness.

A lot of the kids in my houses had troubled backgrounds. Gang leaders and their foot soldiers skulked around the periphery to pass orders to those already in their command and drag the ones who resisted into their murky world. Crime figures always went up in the winter months. There were more robberies, attacks and murders. As the festive season crept closer, cocaine was in high demand too, with middle-class professionals trying to perk up dull dinner parties and city workers sprinkling a little (or a lot of) 'party dust' on their Christmas nights out. The drug gangs were working overtime to ensure supply met demand and they needed vulnerable people to do their dirty work.

The kids in my care were prime targets.

I always knew when the seasons were about to change from autumn to winter because the rose bush in my garden looked depressed. It had been there long before I arrived and long before my family made this house our home. Its roots were knotted into the foundations and its flowers frequented by every bee around. It flourished the rest of the year round, even when it wasn't meant to, facing into the wind, rain and hail defiantly, never bowing to the elements. But as soon as the first hint of winter's chill rippled through the air, ushering out autumn's earthy scent, it would lurch across my garden, slumping as if all of the life had been drained out of it. Its drooping branches always reminded me of someone overwhelmed by a hangover, after they'd spent the night searching the bottom of a bottle for an escape from reality.

Maybe it was the weight of knowing what was to come?

After being a source of life, colour and joy for so long, it knew the darkness was coming. The bleakness and despair of finding nothing in the cold, hard earth to sustain it, until spring returned once more. Perhaps it was too much to bear.

One dark November morning in 2017 I was up early and sipping my third or fourth coffee, fuelling myself with caffeine before I set off to work. Hands still clasped around the warm mug, I peered at the rose bush through the patio windows.

It's gone early this year, I thought.

It was gloomy and damp but not too cold. Winter in London doesn't have the same bite as it did in my childhood back in Halifax. I wondered if the rosebush was a bit of a soft southerner, the kind my friends from home told me I'd turned into over the years.

The early slump was unseasonal enough to grab my attention, momentarily. But I didn't dwell on it.

Looking back, I should probably have recognised it as a sign.

That morning, I drove along the M25 alongside other bleary-eyed commuters, hypnotised by car lights and the rolling grey concrete of the road, and contemplated the change in season. So far, I'd been lucky. The boys in the house were all doing well and had been keeping out of trouble, for the most part. But the mood in the house *had* started to shift. It was almost imperceptible at first. Everything looked the same on the surface, the boys behaving as they always did, but the energy was different – anxious and edgy.

It was a bit like the way you could sense a storm before it arrived.

As I pulled up outside the house – a tall Victorian building in London with a heavy door frame and stained glass windows – I could feel that energy vibrating from the walls of the house, making my hairs stand on end. The house was at full capacity, all eight rooms filled with boys from different backgrounds. For the next two days I was going to be the only member of staff on duty and, although I couldn't quite put my finger on it, something was bubbling just below the surface.

Not that a passer-by would notice.

In fact, I'd have been amazed if anyone who wasn't an immediate neighbour or care worker even realised the house was a semi-independent home. These privately-owned homes always look just like the other houses on the street. That was the confusion. People expected institutional-looking buildings, jail-like even, with bars on the window and beefed-up security to keep the kids safe inside.

Or to keep the kids inside and them safe.

But instead it looked like any other house, warm and welcoming with an immaculately manicured garden. I'd done my best over the months to try to make the atmosphere inside match the external image, to ensure the boys in my care treated the house, the other residents and their neighbours with respect. But even in perfect circumstances there will always be tension among teenage boys. Add conflicting cultures and clashing personalities ebbing and flowing under one roof to the mix and there was bound to be fireworks, at some point.

Logically, I knew being the only staff member on shift could be risky. I knew it wasn't *meant* to happen, if best practice safety processes were being followed. Back when I'd worked in children's homes it would never have happened, because the regulators would have come down on us like a tonne of bricks. But this sector wasn't regulated. John liked to make a profit and less outgoings on staff meant more money for the businesses. I'd done it a few times since starting and my gut told me I could handle whatever happened. After all, John trusted me and I was confident working with kids that came with warning signs, the ones that would send most people running. Gang affiliated, drug addict.

The boys respected me too because I respected them and treated them like equal human beings. I didn't always agree with what they did but I understood they hadn't chosen that life for fun. I knew because I'd once been in their shoes. I'd mixed with gangs as a way to find safety and community when I found myself on the streets and I'd turned to drugs to escape my traumas. These shared experiences gave us some common ground – and a way in for me.

I always walked through the front door holding my breath. Not because I was anxious about the uneasy atmosphere but out of sheer habit. When I'd walked into houses I'd worked in previously, I'd gotten used to almost being knocked off my feet by the most odious stenches.

My body had left those appalling houses, which weren't fit for animals let alone vulnerable young people, but my brain hadn't quite forgotten the smell of rotting food, damp and mould, unwashed clothes and bodies – odours that emanated from every part of the building because those in charge just didn't give a shit. When I raised concerns I'd been told, 'It's better than what they've come from.' The young people had a roof over their head and the company owners got their money from the council and local authorities who placed them there. That was it, end of transaction.

But John's places didn't operate like that at all. I allowed myself to breathe in as I walked through the hall to my office and it smelled clean without being sterile like a dentist's waiting room. I set to work and my concern about tension in the house dissolved as I pored over a mound of paperwork and emails that all needed an urgent response. It was gone

one o'clock before all the boys were up and about, watching TV, talking and preparing food in the kitchen.

It was only between key sessions – the one-to-one meetings where we discussed the boys' progress, perhaps how they were getting on at college, or how they were manging their mental health – that I felt the tension there again, hanging in the air. It was like a tightly wound spring was about to ping loose.

A case of when, not if.

As the hours ticked past and darkness fell, the sensation became even more intense. I started to notice the boys shuffling between rooms and skulking in hallways, set on alert by my presence as I did my rounds.

Something wasn't right. I could smell it in the air. Fear, testosterone, adrenaline, trepidation, anger. A pungent combination that defied description. I knew that I needed to get to the bottom of what was happening.

Heading back into my office, I sat down in front of the screen connected to the cameras set up around the house. I flicked through, one by one, until the living room area appeared on the monitor. A group of the boys were gathered, hunched closely together. It wasn't unusual to see the room busy as it was where they watched TV or did their laundry. But this was different.

Shoulders tight around their ears, two of the boys, Rob and Andrezj, were circling one another, lips snarled and teeth bared. Despite having no sound on the cameras, I could hear their raised voices from across the house as their mouths started to move on the screen.

My stomach sank. This was no social gathering. This was a hair-trigger moment.

The spring was coiled as tight as it could be and it was all about to kick off.

I leapt to my feet and bolted down the corridor, heart already racing as I rounded the corner into the living room. Colourful invective filled the air as the boys squared up to one another.

'Come outside and I'll show you who's a pussy,' hissed Rob.

'Go fuck your mum,' Andrezj snarled back.

Andrezj lunged forward but Rob sidestepped him, smirking as he did. It only served to rile Andrezj even further.

'Guys, what's going on?' I shouted. 'You need to put an end to this right now.'

Was it a row over money? A girl? Gang rivalry?

The possible scenarios rolled around my head as the boys' eyes remained trained on one another. It was as if I wasn't even there. They just carried on staring, stalking one another like prey, as the other boys in the room watched on.

By now, I could feel my heart pounding so hard against my chest that I was certain it was going to burst right out. I was furious.

How dare they disrespect me like this?

But I was scared, too. If the shit hit the fan here, I was fully responsible.

This wasn't like in council-run homes I'd worked in before, where it was a bigger risk if you *did* step in. One report from a kid saying you physically or verbally assaulted them could cost you your career. Here, now, *not* doing something could end in disaster. It was my neck on the line, one way or another. I had to challenge this behaviour and I had to battle to maintain my composure. There was no backup for me to call on and I knew that if I showed fear, I'd lose any shred of control I still had over the situation.

I took a deep breath and put myself between the boys.

'I'm not fucking joking,' I said assertively. 'I don't want any fighting in my house. If you fight, I'll call your social workers and demand you be removed. Now shake hands and leave it at that.'

Countless times, this approach had worked. None of them wanted to end up on the streets in winter. The threat of being removed or having to deal with prying social workers – any more than they had to – was hassle they didn't need.

But not this time.

I still had no idea what had gone on but I was now certain that it was serious. Without so much as glancing at me, the two boys continued to move in ever-decreasing circles towards one another, like hyenas round a carcass. I held my breath as they closed in on me, before forcing my arms out wide.

'No!' I shouted, pushing them both in opposite directions.

I knew I had no option but to escalate my threat.

'Guys, let it go or I call the police.'

Momentarily, it was as if someone had snapped their fingers and broken a spell.

Police.

As soon as the word fell from my lips, their shoulders dropped, the spectators darted and the two antagonists slowly slunk away, still eyeballing one another, unwilling to turn their backs as they retreated to their rooms that were adjacent to one another on the first floor.

Once the room was empty, I exhaled.

Thank fucking God.

I'd seen a few scraps at the house but I'd never felt tension and rage built up like that. I was relieved but not relaxed. Something told me this wasn't over yet. As I made my back to the office, I realised I was biting my nails. It's a dirty habit I detest, especially if people did it in my company. And I *never* did it myself. But my mind was elsewhere. I knew this was the calm before the storm. The low rumble of thunder before lighting struck. Anger like that needed an outlet, it didn't just disappear.

Who is going to make the first move?

Where would it happen?

Should I call the police now, just in case?

It didn't happen often but I needed advice, or at least a second opinion. I picked up my mobile and dialled John's number.

RING, RING. RING, RING. RING, RING . . .

CLICK.

The line went dead and I frowned. Had he just cut me off?

I was about to redial when my phone beeped with a text message from John.

Sorry, Chris. I'm on a boat in the South of France. The reception is bad.

I sucked in my breath angrily and shook my head.

The music is too loud or you're too drunk, more like, I thought.

There was no asking if I was OK, despite the fact I rarely called while on shift, and no offer to try to find a quiet area to call me back. I was on my own. I was in charge and therefore the decision making was all down to me.

I paced my office looking aimlessly at the cameras as the rain hammered like metal pellets against the windowpane. It was as if they had been building up to some loud, explosive crescendo ever since the confrontation in the living room took place.

Then it happened.

Lighting struck.

After a few minutes stewing over whatever had caused the row in the first place, the two boys suddenly burst out of their rooms in attack mode.

When I heard the clatter of first contact, I leapt up so fast that I almost left my skin in my seat. But the time I reached them, they were already intertwined in a heap at the top of the stairs. It was vicious and fast. Kicks launched, punches thrown, biting each other as they rolled around the floor, screaming and screeching obscenities.

It was all fight and no flight.

Suddenly, Andrezj swung for Rob and he wobbled backwards. *Shit. Shit.*

But as the boys tumbled down the stairs, still growling and spitting like animals, I saw my chance and leapt between.

If I can separate them, I might just be able to stop this, I thought.

But the boys had other ideas. Rather than backing off, they kept on going, with me stuck in the middle and taking blows from every direction.

'Stop it, both of you, fucking stop it now!' I shouted, as blood and saliva splattered my face.

I wasn't even sure whose it was.

When we landed on the ground floor, I could taste blood in my mouth and was suddenly aware that my jeans had burst open. I stumbled around trying to pull my trousers up so I could stop the pair of them from beating one another to death but they weren't giving up.

Then it got even worse.

By the time I'd managed to hitch my jeans back up to my waist, I heard the clatter of the locked front door being kicked open and all seven residents of the house spilled out onto the street, screaming, shouting and jumping all over one another.

Blood was splattered on their faces, the walls, pavements and nearby cars.

I was powerless.

There was only one thing I could do. Still holding my jeans around my waist, I ran to the office, grabbed the phone and dialled 999.

'What service do you require?' the operator asked.

'Police,' I said.

I was connected within seconds.

'Listen, I haven't got time for questions and answers. You need to get here quick before someone gets killed,' I said, panic rising in my throat.

Slamming the receiver down, I ran back outside. The scene I was met with was nothing short of a nightmare.

'Stop fighting now,' I screamed.

But my efforts were futile. It was me against seven agitated, volatile young men. To make matters worse, our neighbours were now hanging from their windows. Some were watching, eyes bright with excitement. As if witnessing these troubled young men fight was some kind of blood sport to be revelled in. Others, understandably, were very worried and pissed off local residents. Turns out I wasn't the only one to have called 999.

'I've called the police and I'm going to have you closed down!' yelled one.

'I've got fucking work in the morning, you stupid, fucking feral cunts!' shouted another.

Momentarily, there was a lull in the action and the two main culprits stood toe to toe, exhausted and both bleeding heavily from the nose. I tried to work out what was happening. Three of the boys from the house had sided with Rob, the other two had sided with Andrezj. Were the minority about to concede defeat?

Was it over?

Then I saw it, reflecting a fragment of light from the street lamp above. A knot tightened in my stomach instantly.

A knife . . .

It was held by Marcus, one of the boys who had sided with Andrezj, and had just had quite the pasting. My heart pounded as he carefully concealed the blade from view of his rivals as he edged towards them.

They hadn't seen it, but I had.

Where are the police? I panicked internally.

I felt my breaths quicken as my eyes darted around, trying to figure out a plan. I couldn't have any of the boys getting injured.

Or worse . . .

But before I even had time to gather my thoughts, Marcus raised the knife.

'No!' I shouted.

The lull was over and suddenly everything blurred into one. Arms and limbs flailed as the boys went head to head once again. I lost sight of the knife but I saw some of the boys dash back into the house and return with makeshift weapons to arm themselves with.

My stomach lurched. Someone was going to get stabbed here.

What had I been sitting on?

What had I missed?

How had it ended up here?

I could feel my mouth moving as I shouted at the boys to stop but I couldn't hear the words I was saying, just the blood pounding in my head as I waited for the inevitable to happen.

It was as if I was falling into a dark endless hole, powerless to do anything to stop the nightmare unfolding in front of me.

It was only the sight of flashing blue lights and wail of sirens that pulled me back into the moment. As the squad car screeched onto the pavement, most of the boys scattered, vanishing like ghosts, along with their weapons.

As police officers burst out of the car it was only Rob and Andrezj that remained, locked together and beating the life out of one another. Seeing the police pile onto them was like watching gods emerge from the clouds just in time to stop a bloody catastrophe.

They were arrested and taken away, while everyone in the house had to give a statement. Shaken and duty bound to the young people I looked after, I told the police everything. But the boys closed ranks. The police could find no evidence of weapons and no one was talking.

It was just an argument that got out of hand.

It was only after the police left that I finally got to the bottom of what had caused the fight. Turned out Andrezj had brought some skunk (cannabis) into the house and refused to share with Rob, breaking something of a house tradition. I knew most of the boys smoked weed. If one had some, they'd usually share it with everyone else. While I didn't encourage or allow it openly in the house, I wasn't going to throw the book at them if I caught them. If it was a case of them smoking a joint in their rooms or being out on the streets dealing drugs, I knew where I'd prefer them to be. Technically I should have reported anything like this to their social workers and maybe even the police but working in the private sector and being less tightly regulated allowed me to exercise some discretion. It was all part of my plan to really change up how these kids were treated.

That said, it was the drugs that had led to the fight and I was acutely aware the night could have had a very different ending – one that would have haunted me for the rest of my life.

Once the remaining boys were in bed, I sat in the office with my head in my hands. How had I been so stupid? I'd gotten so wrapped up in my new-found status that I'd completely lost sight of why I was really here. I thought I could handle it all, believed my own hype. The old Chris would never have agreed to work in a house like this alone. In fact, he wouldn't even have agreed to have some of these boys together under the same roof. He'd have understood that their clashing backgrounds would turn the house into a tinderbox, where just one spark could send the whole thing up.

Just like tonight.

I walked to the window and stared out at the blood-splattered pavement. The events of the evening played on a loop in my brain, each time with a new ending more horrific than the last.

Then suddenly, it dawned on me.

I hadn't missed anything. I'd blinded myself to it.

I'd left myself without the support I needed to do my job. I'd put pride before keeping these boys safe. And why?

Money.

Business.
Politics.

I'd become part of the problem. Complicit to the issues in the private sector. I'd drifted from activist and campaigner to business person, playing politics with these boys' lives for more in my bank account. John must have seen my ego a mile off when he met me.

'Chris, I have the money but you have the skills. I'm going to open houses across the country and you're going to run them. You'll be the boss,' he'd said. 'You can handle anything.'

But now I realised that it hadn't been a compliment. It was a challenge he knew I'd take, no matter the risk. I always had to prove myself, it was my biggest downfall. John knew he could play on this so I'd work solo, saving him money on additional staff; so I'd agree to taking in the high-risk residents that he could charge the local authorities top whack for.

The power and pay he could provide had given me a taste of a life that I wanted for myself. I'd seen people with no real experience outside of academia writing reports on how to fix the problems of the care sector and being paid £50,000 a pop for it. It didn't matter that the recommendations were impractical, they got all the glory and I wanted a slice of that – as well as to actually *make* the changes. Not just hypothesise about them.

I had so many ideas about how to revolutionise the sector and I wanted to be the one to implement them – not just where I worked but across the country. John's chain of houses felt like the beginning of that for me. A place where I could trial my approaches before I shared them with the world. But I realised now that I'd been side-tracked from the fundamental reason I'd got into the sector at all: the young people I looked after.

It wasn't about what was best for me, or John, or the business.

It was about what was best for them.

I was angry at myself but I was raging at John, too. I imagined what could have happened if the police hadn't arrived when they did. All I could see was dead bodies all over the street, on my watch. I imagined the story in the local papers: *Care home manager Chris Wild was sentenced to ten years in jail for professional negligence. He will never work with young people again.*

I saw my own body slumped among those in the street and imagined Androulla without a husband and Antonia without a dad. As the anger built inside me, I started to write a resignation letter in my head:

Dear John,

Take your fucking job and stick it up your arse. I didn't come on board to watch a group of kids kill each other because you wouldn't pay for another member of staff and I was too polite to tell you to fuck off.

Yours truly,
Chris

I returned home from my shift the following night slumped as low as my depressed rosebush, weighed down by the fact that I'd allowed myself to be pulled into the failings of the sector and become complicit in a situation that put me and the young people in my care at risk.

This has to stop, I thought.

Not the job, but the failings. Although a part of me wanted to quit, I couldn't. First and foremost, for my family. I had to make a living and I couldn't pile the burden of keeping a roof over our heads on Androulla again, like after I'd left my job in the children's home to try and forge a new path for myself. It wouldn't be fair on her and I didn't want Antonia growing up in a house filled with financial worry. But secondly, I knew I had the opportunity to try and make a change. The semi-independent care sector was a mess. It had been a creeping realisation over a matter of months, but the events of the day had just shone a glaring spotlight on just how much of a mess it was.

After the anger subsided I was filled with another emotion. A sense of responsibility and new-found purpose. I knew there were dark months ahead but for the first time in a long while, I could at least see the issues clearly. I knew that I was becoming part of the problem – the focus on profit over people – and I knew what I had to do to correct it.

CHAPTER TWO
The System

Taylor

I WAS ABOUT TO launch into my rousing 'welcome to your new home' monologue when I noticed his vacant expression and sensed the emptiness in the room. I could tell this was the kind of kid that positivity didn't go down well with, so I decided to keep it factual.

It was a few weeks after John had appointed me into the house manager role and Taylor was my newest resident. At 15 years old, he would be the youngest boy in the house. Legally, we weren't meant to accept under 16s into semi-independent houses but he was two weeks off his birthday and had nowhere else to go, so an exception had been made.

He may have been the youngest but his experience was vast. He'd been in care since he was seven and he had 'the system look' etched all over his face – lines of untold worry carved into his young skin and dark shadows eclipsing any signs of hope. I knew from bitter experience that any words of kindness would bounce off his thick skin, like bullets off titanium.

'Right, Taylor,' I said, passing him a stack of leaflets, 'those are the house rules for you to read. I'll show you to your room.'

He didn't utter a word. Care home kids rarely do at the start. Those moving from the strictly regulated and bureaucratic world of our children's homes into semi-independent care were the toughest nuts to crack. The hardest to reach and help. They'd been institutionalised, to use the technical term – passed from pillar to post and pillow to pillow, with little independence or ability to make choices about their lives. They knew the system inside out and, as much as they hated it, they could use it to their advantage. If you threw the book at them, they'd find ways to recite it straight back at you and tie you up in knots.

Taylor had been read the same house rules a hundred times and more in his short life. He'd heard all the welcome speeches he needed. He'd been put into care for his own safety, a victim of domestic violence from a young age. He was an emotional and physical punching bag for his parents, whose unfortunate life choices had led to mental health issues and addiction. He was better off in the system than facing a life of neglect at home. Not that it was the perfect solution. Far from it.

He'd been passed up and down the length of the country. More than 16 moves in nearly eight years. Bad placements, personality clashes and financial issues with local authorities – it wasn't Taylor's fault. Those were all things that the system, our processes and procedures, was meant to iron out. But it rarely did. The damage it caused was almost irreparable. It was like sending a fragile parcel in the post with no protective packaging and booting it from destination to destination. Each time it arrived more shattered and with sharper edges, making it harder to pick up and put back together.

As we trudged up the stairs in silence, I was trying to muster up some sense of positivity. But I'd been here so many times with kids just like Taylor. I'd offered support and kindness and been told to fuck off. I'd tried discipline and been told to fuck off. I'd tried to welcome them into a home and . . . You get the picture.

Already feeling defeated, I swung open the door to Taylor's room. I always went the extra mile to make sure the boys had a nice clean room. Each one had a bed with a nice set of sheets, a few picture frames from IKEA, a side cabinet and a lamp; it was simple but immaculate. However, I sensed Taylor was about to have an opinion. He looked around the room slowly then scrunched up his face into an expression I couldn't read.

Disgust? Anger? Indifference?

'What's up, mate?' I said. 'Don't you like it?'

He shook his head and then I heard his voice for the first time. 'The room's great,' he said quietly. 'I– I'm just surprised.'

'About what?' I asked.

'The bed,' he said, nodding towards it.

'What about it?' I asked, puzzled.

'It's made. I've never had my bed made before,' he said, his voice cracking slightly. 'The sheets look new and everything.'

I swallowed the golf ball-sized lump rising in my throat.

'They are, mate,' I said. 'Haven't you just left a children's home? Didn't they give you fresh bedclothes there?'

Taylor shook his head. 'Nah. I just had a mattress on the floor,' he said, nonchalantly.

As if it was a perfectly normal thing for any child to endure.

I was losing my fight with the ball of sadness pushing up from inside me, tears pricking my eyes. How was this still happening? I'd been in a children's home in 1992 and it was bad then – physical abuse, conditions that weren't fit for animals and a reign of fear that kept a whole catalogue of abuse hidden behind closed doors for decades. But we were almost 20 years on. Why had so little changed? Why were children still being treated like stray dogs and existing on scraps?

I bit inside my lip to try and hold it back but as the metallic taste of blood filled my mouth, I knew I had to make my excuses.

'Be back in a minute, mate,' I said, patting him gently on the back. 'Make yourself at home.'

Then I quickly turned my head so he couldn't see me welling up and blindly stumbled away, not quite sure exactly where I was going. I found myself halfway down the stairs before I managed to compose myself. Taylor's response to something so simple, so trivial – a clean, freshly made bed – had shattered me emotionally.

How had this child gone 15 years without *anyone* showing him such a small mark of kindness? Not his mum or dad, not his foster carers, not even those at the children's home into whose care he'd been placed at seven years old. For fuck's sake. Even Taylor's social worker hadn't been bothered to drop him off at the house and provide him with proper representation. He'd rolled up alone at 9.30pm in a taxi stuffed with black binbags containing his belongings. He was like a rabbit in the headlights, no idea what was awaiting him this time.

At this new house.

In this new town.

With these new people.

Again.

It was no wonder that his paperwork documented countless times he'd been abusive towards staff members, smashed up his room and gone missing. Why would he demonstrate respect, love and consideration when he'd never been shown any in his life?

As I drove home that night, Taylor's reaction to the bed played over and over in my mind, along with the things he'd told me about the homes he'd been in before. By the time I stepped through my front door, the tears were welling in my eyes again. But this time, safe in my own home, I didn't have to hold back.

Androulla stepped into the hall and took one look at me.

'Chris, what's wrong?' she said, instinctively taking me into her arms.

'It's this new kid at the house . . . ' I started.

As the story flooded from my lips, tears poured from my eyes.

'What's going on?' I said. 'How can this be happening? How is it still happening?'

Androulla knew this wasn't just about Taylor, it was my own trauma bubbling to the surface. My own experience of living in Skircoat Lodge in Halifax and the ghosts of all the kids I'd seen destroyed by the inhumanity of the place. The abuse I'd seen might have been curbed by regulation but those places were still scarring children by failing to be the one thing they were meant to be. Children's *homes*.

A home.

Safe, secure and with the basics you need to feel human. Like a bloody made bed. *Not just a mattress on the floor.*

Lots of the kids who came into the houses that John owned had some experience of being loved. Even if it was many years ago, in a different city or even country. But not Taylor. He had never had a family holiday, Christmas with his parents or a hug from his mum when he wasn't feeling well.

It left him desensitised to any kind of affection from anyone.

Even the relationships he tried to build were snatched away. He started a relationship with a girl in one of the houses in London that he'd lived in, so they moved him 100 miles across the country to prevent them from seeing each other. The care home managers couldn't let the relationship continue under their roof, obviously, but tearing up any shallow roots that Taylor had planted wasn't the answer.

Every time they moved him, he ran back to the city to see her.

Every time they moved him, he lost that little bit more hope in the system.

Until there was nothing left at all.

He didn't know it because his heart had never been cared for, but it was broken. It had never captured any beauty or felt love. I imagined the vibrant, red blood pumping around his body discolouring over time, as hope and emotion drained out of him, turning from brown to grey to a gradient shade of black. And so I vowed to do everything I could to convince Taylor that there were people who cared. To break down his barriers so he could start to mend his broken heart. And the work started straight away.

I showered him with praise for every positive thing he did. From joining the rest of the house to watch TV in the lounge to washing his dinner plates. Nothing went unnoticed or unrewarded. But Taylor never responded. My words bounced straight off his defence shield.

'You could say thank you, it won't hurt you,' I said one day, exasperated.

'What am I meant to be thankful for?' he snapped.

'You have a roof over your head, a nice bedroom and you're surrounded by people who care about you,' I said, gently.

Taylor narrowed his eyes and shot me a look that could have turned me to stone, like Medusa.

'I don't need anyone to care for me, OK?' he hissed. 'I've been on my own for as long as I can remember and I've survived.'

I tried to speak but I was frozen. Held in suspended animation as Taylor grimaced.

'Checkmate,' he said, before turning and walking back to his room.

One nil to Taylor, I thought.

I was impressed he'd used a chess reference for his '*touché*' moment but if he thought I was giving up, he had another think coming. I'd always known this was going to be a challenge. What Taylor didn't know was that I wasn't like the rest. I didn't stop playing when someone called checkmate and I wasn't going to quit at the first hurdle. But with Taylor, the hurdles just kept coming.

He knew he was safe for two more years. Even if this placement broke down, the authorities would have to move him somewhere else. And what was one more move to him? I viewed it differently. I knew that in two years' time, when he turned 18, the support would stop. He wouldn't be able to remain in my house because the council wouldn't continue to support him. Only young people with the most complicated additional needs are supported past 18. Physical disabilities, severe mental health issues and learning disabilities. There's a finite amount of resource available and it tends to go to the most at risk. That doesn't mean that those who don't get help don't need it, it just means that they can't get it because there's no budget to support it. At 18, Taylor would have to go and find himself somewhere to live independently. If he couldn't do that there were charities who might be able to assist but even that wasn't guaranteed if he hadn't laid the groundwork, found a job or got into education. If he hadn't worked out how he was going to pay rent, his difficult life would get even harder. He'd be out on his ear with nowhere to turn and there was nothing I'd be able to do about it then.

I didn't want to see that so I attempted every tactic in the book with him.

They all failed.

He was impervious to kindness, he laughed in the face of discipline and he rejected any offer of support or even a listening ear. In his mind, he'd seen and heard it all before and he wasn't about to fall for it again.

But still we kept on. The persistence of me and my team baffled and frustrated him. We didn't respond in the ways he was used to. When he screamed down from his room one night, threatening to smash it up, we didn't respond with anger or aggression. We didn't storm up the stairs and take a heavy-handed approach.

'Anything you break, you pay for,' I called up.

'What?' he yelled back, sounding genuinely stumped.

'You break it, you pay for it,' I said. 'Now calm down.'

'Argh!' he screamed through gritted teeth, stamping his foot like an insolent child. 'Why are you not hating me?'

I sucked in a slow, sad breath. That was all he expected from anyone. For them to hate him.

'Why would I?' I responded.

Then I walked away.

Patience had always been key to me forging a career in the care sector. The kids I worked with needed time and I had plenty of it. But there was still always a tipping point. Too little patience and you'd explode, too much and you start to let go.

As the weeks and months passed, I stayed patient but nothing was changing. Taylor wasn't letting any of us in. He simply swung from sullen silence to angry outbursts. It was one of the latter that finally got to me. I'd been trying to talk to him, see how he was getting on and encourage him to engage in one of our key work sessions.

'You can see me as a friend,' I'd said. 'Not just a professional.'

Innocuous as it sounds, to him it was like I'd held a match to a firework.

Taylor went off.

'I don't want to be your friend, I don't want your support, I just want you to leave me the fuck alone!' he exploded.

So I did. I put my hands up and walked away. I could only try so much.

If he didn't want my help, I wasn't going to waste any more of my time and energy; I decided to maintain my professional duty of care to Taylor and nothing more. After that, he was never a problem. We relaxed into a sad state of indifference.

Well, almost.

He only really left his room to cook himself the same 49-pence frozen pizza he bought every day from the local corner shop. I dreaded to think what was in it. Or what wasn't, more to the point – the kid was going to end up with scurvy.

I decided to get him a bag of fruit. I didn't expect a thank you or even any acknowledgement. This wasn't me trying to win him over. I was simply doing my job, delivering on a basic requirement to ensure his health and wellbeing.

I dropped the bag of fruit outside his door.

The next day it was still there.

And the next.

I even saw him step over it on his way out to the shop.

In the end, as the fruit started to wither and brown, Ardian, a refugee from Albania, knocked on the door.

'If you don't want this, may I have it?' he asked.

'Of course, take it,' Taylor said, before closing his door again.

It wasn't just me he shut out, it was his housemates too. When they tried to strike up a conversation he was always polite but he ended it quickly.

'Hey, man. How's it going?' the boys would call to him.

'Good,' he'd reply, walking away.

The more he pulled away from me, the clearer it had become to me. This was how he protected himself. He pushed everyone away to avoid being hurt. His survival mechanism was isolation. It was all he knew.

Even though many would have seen him as a lost cause, I just *couldn't* give up on him, even when I tried. That moment on the day he'd arrived kept playing over and over in my head. The moment he'd seen that made bed. That glimmer of hope, joy, appreciation . . . whatever it was. It was *there*.

Maybe *that* was the key? To help him to feel valued and worthwhile *to himself* . . .

The government puts money aside for kids in care for every year they are in the system. When they move into semi-independent provision at 16, they are allowed to access it under the supervision of their social workers and house managers. It isn't much, but it is *theirs*.

I wasn't helping him. He wasn't leaning on me. He was depending on himself. I was just a facilitator because I legally had to be. I explained my plan to John and submitted the paperwork to Taylor's social worker that would give me permission to take him out for the day. A week after making my request, I took Taylor to Bluewater Shopping Centre. It was an excruciating four hours; he barely said two words as we shopped. But he seemed content enough buying himself new trainers, tracksuits, baseball caps and some bits for his bedroom. After he was done, we grabbed some food at an all-you-can-eat Chinese buffet in the centre.

We made our trips to the counter and came back, plates piled high, laughed and ate like kings.

'That was the best Chinese meal I have ever had,' I said, holding my stomach after I finished my last mouthful. 'I'm stuffed.'

Then, finally, the ice started to thaw. Taylor looked up and nodded in agreement, a satisfied smile dancing across his face.

'Thank you,' he said.

And there it was, completely out of the blue. That glimmer of hope again. I'd finally broken through the walls he put around himself and a crack of light was gleaming out.

So I kept chipping away. Helping Taylor to help himself. Being there for him, in a way that he didn't feel was a threat. In the weeks that followed, something changed in him. I found myself getting reports from my team that he was talking more and engaging in conversations.

Taylor watched TV in the lounge with us today.

I saw Taylor chatting to Tomo outside.
Taylor made me a cup of tea this morning!

I think my heart could have just about burst with joy. It had taken four months, but we had done it. We had broken down Taylor's barriers and now we could start to make progress. He was too young to hate the world and I wanted him to give it a chance. I didn't want this to be the end of the road for him, the last bastion of safety and security before he was left to fend for himself at 18.

I wanted this to be his new beginning.

On paper, that's exactly what moving into semi-independent supported accommodation should be. A new beginning. These unregulated provisions should be a bridge from leaving institutional care and a stepping stone towards independence and a better life.

For many children, it is the right choice. But only if it's done right. And that's the problem, it rarely is. The system is plagued with problems. When children living in care homes have to move on at the age of 16, there are a number of options. For children with complex needs that require ongoing full-time support, for example, mental health issues, autism or physical disabilities, there are specialist homes that are regulated by the Care Quality Commission (CQC). For the rest, there are foster homes or the unregulated provisions like the ones that I worked in, where we provided support, rather than 'care'.

Looks straightforward, right? A clear path for any child need-
ing post-16 support, whether they've been brought up in the
British care system or arrived in the country seeking asylum.

It's not.

First of all, what does 'care' mean? What does it look like
in practice? What qualifies someone to need 'care' after the
age of 16? It's not defined in law anywhere, leaving it open to
interpretation. Terms like 'complex needs' also have no clear
definitions. It's not just determined by the age of the child,
although that is a factor. It's about the child's vulnerability
and the level of help they need, how often they need it and
who will deliver it.

Alongside problems with definitions lies demand. In 2016/17
there were approximately 96,000 'looked after' children – another
term for children in care that encompasses those in regulated and
unregulated provisions – in the UK. In England, the number of
looked after children has increased every year since 2008. These
year-on-year increases in the number of kids puts the system as
it was intended to function, and all its processes, under immense
and ever-growing pressure.

The needs of these children are varied, of course, from those
who have come from abusive homes to those who have fled
war-torn foreign lands. The already creaking system bends and
bows as it is required to deliver 'care' to young people who have
been sexually abused or trafficked thousands of miles from their
homes, or who are living with PTSD or crippling physical conditions. There just aren't enough places in registered children's

homes or other facilities providing specialist regulated care to meet demand.

Supply is falling too. Austerity has seen local government budgets cut by more than half between 2010 and 2019.[1] Public care homes that are run by local authorities are being sold off at an alarming rate – and being snapped up by private companies. In fact, a 2020 report documented that more than three quarters (77 per cent) of looked after children were placed in private settings instead of provisions run by housing associations, local authorities or charities.[2] They've been stripped to the bone and it's our most vulnerable kids who pay the price because this is where our 'straightforward' system falls apart.

The lack of 'care' providers means that kids who really need that level of support end up in unregulated provisions that can't deliver the help they need, because there is simply nowhere else to put them. Local authorities scramble not to find the *right* placement for the child in question but *any* placement that fits the budget. Often they don't even bother to inspect where they're sending children. Whether that's due to lack of time or interest is irrelevant. They take the concept of 'care' and shape it to fit what they need it to. The paperwork I've seen over the years is clear evidence of this, information often conspicuous by its absence.

---

[1] www.centreforcities.org/reader/cities-outlook-2019/a-decade-of-austerity/

[2] www.gov.uk/government/publications/looked-after-children-in-independent-or-semi-independent-placements

For example, social workers are handed cases with young people who are affiliated with gangs. They are desperate to place them, so they leave that information off the referral, making the child infinitely easier to place, especially when that child comes with a handsome price tag. But three months down the line the provision that took the lucrative placement will have a house full of vulnerable young people all groomed into county lines (see Chapter 4). In a way, it's a bit like buying your dream house. It's the one you want and it's the perfect price, but the estate agent 'forgets' to tell you about the gruesome murder that happened in the bedroom where your children will be sleeping. Sales, that's what it has become. Omitting information to seal the deal, then arguing they did it for the right reasons.

As public provisions are stripped away, it's the private companies that become the big winners. They know how desperate local authorities are to place the seemingly never-ending stream of broken children somewhere, *anywhere*, to take them off their hands. And they know they'll pay because no matter how big the bill, it's cheaper than running a provision themselves.

As a result, 73 per cent of the sector is privately run and not subject to the 'checks and balances' we see in other, regulated settings.[3] And of course, where there is profit to be made, there's always cost-cutting, corruption and a cold and callous approach to the value of human life. Each child comes with a

---

[3] https://www.bbc.co.uk/news/uk-54093367

price tag. The bigger their problems, the higher the price and the bidder who can offer everything for nothing, preferably the fastest, will get the tender.

Kids being traded like cattle at auction.

The semi-independent care sector claims to provide support and a bridge from care into living independently but these homes are first and foremost businesses, with kids as currency. And those at the top, those trading in human lives, well, they reap the rewards. These private companies seek only to make money off looked after children, regardless of what their slick websites filled with fuzzy feelgood stories suggest. And because they're not beholden to any regulating body, it's easy. They can have kids sleeping on mattresses with no bedding, running away and surviving off corner shop pizzas because no one comes to check, not really.

And the councils? Well, they place these young people in shitholes because the law says they can. For local authorities and the private care home owners it's win-win. Social workers can clear another case file from their desks and the owners of private homes can line their pockets. As the business transaction takes place, the welfare of the child slips through the cracks.

What compounds the issue, when children arrive in semi-independent care from children's homes, is that the system has already failed them. Regulation by Ofsted means they have been kept safer than kids in care in the 1970s and 1980s, when child sex exploitation, physical and emotional abuse was rife.

But they're still not homes. They are still neglected and forgotten. Their needs are not met.

I have seen it with my own eyes. In the early days of my career, I worked in some dreadful children's homes. I had to take the work to gain the experience I needed to progress to a place where I could actually make a difference. What's more, while I was writing *Damaged*, I had to put food on my family's table too, so I wasn't in a position to say no. But I could see clearly how the system was letting the kids down. All I could do then was the best for those kids I was responsible for. But as my career progressed, I became able to pick and choose where I wanted to work. Places that I believed had the children's needs at heart. I vowed never to work anywhere I wouldn't want to live myself.

I tried to be the change I wanted to see.

There were – and still are – some care workers trying to make a difference but it's mainly the old guard doing the bare minimum while they wait to retire, young graduates who churn through jobs unable to deal with the pressure and realities that their university degree did not warn them about and minimum wage workers, for whom the hassle of giving a fuck just isn't worth it.

Taylor was a direct product of that system. It was as if it had drained every bit of hope. He was used to people giving up on him at the first hurdle and he was accustomed to disappointment. He honestly felt like no one gave a shit about him. After all, his social worker hadn't even bothered to bring him to his new home, had he?

The day after he arrived at the home, I spoke to Taylor's social worker and I asked why he'd not come with him to make sure he arrived safely. I wish I could tell you that he'd had an emergency, that's why he couldn't make it. But that wasn't the case.

'Yeah, sorry about that, mate. The wife booked a fancy restaurant and I couldn't be late. I'd lose my promise, you know?' he said. I could *hear* the sleazy 'nudge-nudge, wink-wink' motion he was definitely doing at his end.

'Not really,' I said, my teeth clenched. 'The kid's 15. He should have been escorted here. At *any* time, but especially so late at night.'

'Won't happen again,' he said.

But I knew it would. Livid, I reported him to his line manager but nothing came of it. In fact, she never even replied.

That's why I didn't blame Taylor for being so angry at the world. His life experience had left scars on his heart and it was easier for him to make people hate him so they wouldn't try to help him than risk another person proving they didn't give a shit and walking away or passing him on.

Some care home kids respond well when they realise living in supported accommodation is different to life in a strictly regulated care home. They develop the skills they need and they move on in life. I wish I could tell you Taylor was one of them but after he left the house, we lost contact. That's the hardest part of the job – the outcome. The gratification of finding out someone made it through might not come for years. In fact, it might never come at all because you simply never find out what happened to them after they left your care. And the saddest fact about many leaving the system at 18 is that the outcome often isn't a positive one. Some flourish and grow out of the adversity they've faced. But for many looked after children, semi-independent care is a stepping stone not to independence but to a bleak future.

In its current state, it's not fit for purpose for too many and that *has* to change.

CHAPTER THREE

Seeking Refuge

Yonah

SOME YOUNG PEOPLE DON'T care about the quality of support they receive, who they live with or where they live. When they arrive in a new place, it's just another move to them. They are the direct result of a system that has churned them through house, after house, after house.

Lost souls with no roots and no hope.

Then there are the ones who come from such abject poverty or who have experienced horrors that we could never even begin to comprehend. They'd never had anything so they appreciate absolutely everything. Yonah was one of those children.

I don't think I'd ever seen a human being look so ill and still be breathing until the first time I met him. He was stood next to his social worker, who was decked out in full PPE. It looked a bit much but there was probably a good reason. I didn't need telling that Yonah was a refugee: the bones pushing through his skin wrote that story on his body. I guessed he was from Africa, a continent whose refugees often arrived riddled with diseases like tuberculosis or hepatitis, and Yonah certainly looked like he could be ill. His hair was knotted and thick with dirt and he must have been wearing the same clothes for weeks. I saw the filth caked underneath his long nails and shuddered. It was probably soil from Calais' infamous refugee camps.

And whatever else he'd had to drag himself through to get here.

As his chest rose and fell weakly, I could smell the decay of his teeth escaping on his breath. Obviously, kids like Yonah who enter the country as refugees or seeking asylum haven't had access to simple things like washing facilities or a tooth-brush on their arduous journeys. You'd think, being the First World country that we are, there'd be something provided to them when they got here.

But that's not how it works.

Yonah had arrived in the UK on a Friday and been taken straight to a local police station, where he'd been left in a cell while the local authorities got their shit together. Of course, with it being a weekend, that meant nothing happened until Monday. At that point it was all go.

John got the phone call at 6am on the Monday morning but I knew nothing about it until I arrived at the house to start my shift at 9am. When I pulled up outside and saw John's car parked nearby, I felt a knot tighten in the pit of my stomach. He usually only turned up if something was drastically wrong. I steeled myself as I walked through the door, my mind trip-ping through the horrors that might await.

An assault, arrest . . . or a suicide?

58

As I stepped inside, I was greeted by John bowling down the corridor with a brand new duvet and pillow set in his arms, the house buzzing with activity.

'We have an emergency placement coming, from a *new* local authority,' he said, dragging the word 'new' out for emphasis.

I exhaled discreetly as relief washed over me. Now it made sense.

A new placement from a new local authority was the private care sector equivalent of an unplanned fire drill or a surprise quiz at school. It could be a test and if you did well, you *might* be rewarded. Once they see how organised and prompt you can be, how you can respond at a moment's notice and are willing to take *any* kind of placement they put your way, that's when you shoot up to the top of their tender list.

It was a *very* lucrative opportunity.

'Who is this new placement?' I asked. 'Where do they come from?'

John flapped his arm at me dismissively. 'I don't have a clue. They called me this morning asking if I could take someone and I said yes,' he said. 'Now, you make sure we look after him because if we do, we'll get loads more work from them.'

I bit my lip and smiled through clenched teeth. 'Of course, John,' I said. 'We always look after our kids.'

I liked John and – fair play to him – he did insist on far higher standards than lots of semi-independent provisions I'd seen. But that wasn't entirely selfless. He was a businessman first. Being a safe, comfortable and flexible home were selling points. Potential risks to other residents, things that could upset the finely balanced ecosystem of the house when a new person arrived, he didn't give two hoots about.

That was my problem to sort out.

I'd barely had time to catch my breath when Yonah and his social worker arrived. She'd driven to the police station first thing, collected him and then driven two hours to our house.

As he shuffled through the hall, Yonah kept his face buried in his hands, following the sound of our feet as he shook violently, like a scared dog. I gently guided him to a seat at the kitchen table, terrified that his spindly legs would give way. It was only when he sat down that he dropped his hands to the tabletop and stared at me, wide-eyed and terrified. His face was pale and gaunt and the whites of his eyes jaundiced. He was so frail that he honestly looked like he might drop dead at any minute.

If not from malnutrition or illness, then from fear, I thought.

'Don't be afraid, mate,' I soothed, breathing through my mouth to prevent the putrid smell from entering my nostrils. 'You're safe here.'

'He doesn't speak English,' the social worker snapped, tapping her foot impatiently.

She clearly has somewhere else to be.

As I discreetly opened the windows in the kitchen to better ventilate the room as it became thick with the odour of Yonah's travels, he spoke.

'No money, no food,' he said, as he rubbed his belly to indicate he was hungry.

I spun on my heel and glared at the social worker. 'Please tell me you got him some food?' I said.

She'd driven for two hours, past countless service stations and supermarkets. The boy looked half-dead. Surely from the moment she'd seen him, getting him something to eat and drink would have been a priority?

Apparently not.

'I have some money for *you* to get him some bits,' she replied, looking at me like I was something on her shoe as she passed me a small white envelope.

I curled my lip in disgust as I fought the urge to snatch it angrily from her hands. She knew damn well she should have gotten him some food, she just couldn't be bothered. And she didn't like me pulling her up on it.

'You're going to need to make an appointment with the dentist and the doctors. Then you'll need to arrange his placement meeting and an official health check. That will need to be done this week, obviously,' she said, trying to get one over on me.

'I'm aware of the process,' I said firmly.

'Good,' she said. 'Are we done here?'

'We are,' I said curtly. 'Thank you.'

As much as I enjoyed a bit of sport, baiting social workers who didn't do their job properly out of choice – as opposed to those that tried but couldn't, because of budget cuts and under-staffing – I had important work to do with our new resident.

'I'm Chris,' I said, poking my chest with my fingers. 'Chris.'

Yonah mimicked my actions.

'Yonah,' he said.

'I'm going to make you some food,' I said, putting my hand to my mouth.

A smile spread across his face, exposing his cracked and rotten teeth. The poor thing needed to see a dentist and a doctor as soon as I could manage. In the rush of the morning, I hadn't had a chance to get out to do a shop but I had some leftover pasta that I'd made for my lunch in the fridge, so I tipped it into a bowl and put it in front of him.

I turned to get him a fork, but by the time I got to the drawer Yonah was already scooping up the starchy tubes with his dirty hands and swallowing them down whole. My chest felt like a pressure cooker as my anger towards the social worker continued to build. What would it have taken to grab the boy a bag of crisps or a sandwich? He'd been stuck alone in a cold police cell, probably too afraid to eat, for 48 hours. It's the least she could have done.

Once Yonah cleared his plate, I gave him a glass of water and one of the local shop's 'no frills' chocolate biscuits. John would never let me buy branded varieties with the house budget because he thought they were a waste of money.

Yonah held it up and gasped, like he was examining a rare treasure.

'Tank you. Tank you. Tank you, Chris,' he said.

He was clearly exhausted, so once he'd eaten I took him to his room and gave him some fresh towels.

'Tank you. Tank you. Tank you, Chris,' he said again, over and over.

'Please, you don't have to thank me,' I said. 'You get some sleep and when you wake up, we'll do some food shopping.'

I don't think he understood a word I was saying but I tried my best to make him feel comfortable. Once he was safely in his room, I went to my office to look at the limited paperwork I'd been given for him and to call the British Red Cross to see if they had any more information from the camps in Calais.

His story had less meat on the bone than he did. All we knew was he was from Eritrea and he was believed to be 17 years old. If that information was right – ages and dates of birth are often disputed during an asylum claim – then that meant we had a year to get his asylum claim approved and prepare him to live independently. Twelve months to get him through all of the Home Office's red tape.

It was no time at all. But if we didn't, he could be sent straight back to Eritrea.

As he settled into the house, it was Yonah himself that revealed more about his journey. We talked for hours over endless cups of tea. Although he'd only been in the UK a matter of weeks, his journey here had started years earlier.

'I left home at 13 years old,' he said. 'No work, no food. Only army, bad government.'

'You left to escape the bad government?' I asked.

'Yes, and army,' he replied.

When I found out where he was from, I did my research. Eritrea is a small country on the Red Sea, bordered by Sudan,

Djibouti and Ethiopia. Yonah had been born into a war zone. Since 1998, it had been torn apart by unrest and conflict. Of its population of 5.3 million people, more than 480,000 had been forcibly displaced. Its totalitarian government had been in place for 25 years and there were no elections, no constitution and no independent press.

What they *did* have was compulsory national service.

At 16, when young people in the UK are playing football with friends or learning the latest TikTok dance, Eritrean teenagers are being forced to spend their final year of second-ary education in a notorious military camp known as *Sawa*. In fact, for the best part of two decades, children were taken straight from school, handed a rifle with orders to kill and sent out onto the frontline of the country's war with Ethiopia.

On paper, following an 18-month service they were free to leave, but in reality these youngsters were being conscripted for life. Corrupt military commanders extended the service indefi-nitely, trapping thousands on a bloody battlefield. There were only two choices for Yonah and his peers: serve and try to sur-vive. Or try to leave.

Yonah's family had chosen the latter.

The odds were stacked on either side. If you made it through the war, you might be released from your duties and allowed to live your life. But what chances did you have in a war that had already raged for 20 years? When food was scarce and your enemies weren't just the opposing side but the military officials you served, subjecting you to torture, violence, religious repres-sion, sexual harassment and exploitation?

But the likelihood of escaping was slim too. The country's borders with Ethiopia and Sudan were patrolled by guards who were told to shoot to kill and take no prisoners. But if death was the only escape from the nightmare of the country's military service, surely the dream of finding a better life was worth the risk?

'I knew that everyone had to go to the army,' he said. 'But I didn't want to kill or be killed.'

His family scraped together as much money as they could to get Yonah out of Eritrea. Yonah managed to clear the border into Sudan, where he was met by the men who would provide his route to safety. But the escape route was organised gangs of human traffickers.

'I didn't know where I was going when they took me,' Yonah said. 'They blindfolded me and I thought I was going to die.'

I watched as he sank back inside himself before my eyes, the memories wrapping around his arms like tentacles, pulling him back in time four years. The fear was still just as fresh.

Once in Sudan, they were met by another gang who took the small group, which was predominately made up of children, through the Sahara Desert. Yonah was taken one way, with the boys, while the girls were taken elsewhere. It was only later that Yonah discovered they most likely ended up being trafficked into the sex trade.

With every change of hands and at every border, a ransom had to be paid from the funds his family had given him. Until eventually they arrived in Libya, where Yonah's nightmare really began.

The perils of the route were well known to the Eritrean community. Once they set foot in Libya, they'd be arrested, kidnapped for ransom or detained in cramped compounds run by the Libyan soldiers or the rebel Toubou tribe, which had a successful cross-border trade in black market goods and drugs.

And people.

From here there were only two ways out. For your family to pay the extortionate ransom fee – not an option for most – or to do as your captors told you, until you worked to pay off your 'debt' and buy your freedom.

If you lasted long enough, that is.

Yonah was detained at the Al Sabaa Detention Centre in Tripoli, which had a brutal reputation and was filled with evil and pain. There were no limits to the demands of those in control at Al Sabaa.

'I had come so far but I was sad and very scared for my life,' he said.

'What happened there?' I asked, gently.

'The prison officers would strip us naked and march us outside,' he said, hands trembling. 'They would put us in a line and tell us to stay still so they could put their empty beer bottles on our heads.'

I frowned. *Why would they—*

Yonah read the confusion on my face.

'Then they lift their rifles and started to shoot,' he said, raising his hand, fingers bent into a gun shape. 'Bang, bang, bang.'

Used for target practice.

I blinked back tears that suddenly pricked the corners of my eyes as I imagined the fear that Yonah must have felt, eyes squeezed tight, willing every muscle in his body to freeze, knowing even a ripple of skin could mean the difference between life and death.

'I was always lucky, but some were not. Sometimes I saw my friends being dragged away screaming in pain.' He paused. 'Or not making any sound at all. I never saw them again.'

For two years, he endured physical violence at the hands of his captors. Others, he said, were sexually abused or just disappeared altogether. But finally, he and another youth, who had become his best friend, were able to pay for their freedom. They left the shores of Libya in a tiny boat packed with other refugees, all desperate to cross the Mediterranean Sea to Calais. It was the penultimate leg of Yonah's journey, but not his friend's.

'A storm came,' Yonah said. 'The boat was very small and it was thrown up by the waves. My friend, he fell into the sea.'

'Did they go back for him?' I said.

'I shouted and pointed,' he said. 'I said, "My friend is in the water!" But they ignored me.'

After travelling thousands of miles over two years, defying all those odds of survival, Yonah's friend's journey ended there, in a watery grave.

'They left him to drown. They left many to drown,' he said.

In Calais, Yonah met the British Red Cross, who gave him some assistance. He was so close to his safe haven that he could see it. The blurry haze of Dover across the Channel.

'It was like I could almost touch it,' he said. 'But to get there was not easy.'

He was so close, yet so far.

After a year in the refugee camp at Calais, he once again turned to criminal gangs. With no legal structure in place and the French and English governments reluctant to take any responsibility for the asylum seekers in Calais, he risked being stuck there for life if he didn't find a way to get to England. So, cramped into the back of a lorry, with others whose tales were as desperate as his own, he finally made it here.

'I am here but I am still scared for my life now,' he said in his broken English.

'Why? You're safe here,' I said.

'Only if I can stay,' he replied.

I couldn't shake the haunted look in his eyes as he said those words. Yonah knew as well as I did that although his physical journey was over, he had another one to navigate. The road to his right to stay in the UK.

Once again, the odds weren't in his favour. And if this was where his luck ran out, he could be deported back to Eritrea.

I managed to get him registered with a local GP quickly, raising my concerns about his health as I was worried for Yonah, but also for the other boys in the house and me and my staff members as well. He was inoculated and had all the necessary tests done. When his blood tests came back they showed he was positive for tuberculosis but it wasn't active so he wasn't infectious or as ill as I had feared. A course of strong antibiotics for three months was prescribed and, as his health returned, we began to start the real fight.

As a newly arrived asylum seeker, Yonah was given a place to live, access to education, £58 a week to live on – like his peers who had arrived at the house through the British care system – and legal representation for his Home Office claim. The first stage of that claim was getting his application registration card or 'ARC'. It was a credit card-sized piece of plastic issued by the Home Office to individuals claiming asylum, containing information about the holder's identity, their nationality and age and if their given age was being disputed as part of the claim.

It looked like nothing but it was everything.

Without an ARC, Yonah couldn't access health or dental care outside of his urgent, initial check-up. He couldn't try to find a job, get a bus pass or open a bank account. He couldn't even walk in the street without getting arrested.

The ARC was his key to starting his new life.

But until he had it in his hands, he was in limbo. A prisoner in the house, incarcerated by the bureaucracy of our system. At first, the wait didn't matter. He was just happy to be in a safe place with a roof over his head. After years of sleeping on dirty floors, he took pride in his bedroom and kept it immaculately clean.

Hailing from a deeply Christian country, Yonah was both God-fearing and God-trusting. He tried to live a good life and had no interest in the material trappings of expensive phones, clothes and trainers that turned the heads of his housemates. He never said it, because he was a nice, kind boy, but I sensed he found such displays of wealth a little vulgar, sinful even, perhaps.

He'd lived a life of destitution, so suddenly having £58 a week to his name was like winning the lottery. Especially since now his money didn't immediately need to pass to the hands of the next set of traffickers, on the next leg of his journey.

Yonah knew how to budget and how to cook.

Boy, did he know how to cook.

I could always tell when he had received his allowance. I'd walk into the house and the scent of cumin would drift through the hall, enticing me towards the kitchen. Yonah would be standing near the hob, stirring the biggest pot we had in the house. If he heard you enter the room, he'd turn, smile and wipe the back of his hand across his forehead, inevitably smudging tomato sauce or flour across his face.

'I make food for the house, Chris,' he said. 'A family dish. From home. My mother taught me.'

'Nice one, mate,' I'd say, giving him the thumbs up. 'Smells good.'

He was like an apothecarist, mixing herbs and spices in such a way that drew the boys from every corner of the house, bringing them around the table to tuck into a delicious bowl of *tsebhi*, a spicy stew that could be made with lamb, mutton or ground beef, served with a flatbread called *injera*. A pot of the stuff could last for days and he gave it away gladly, expecting nothing in return.

Yonah enrolled at the local college on a basic course for English speakers of other languages (ESOL) and excelled in his classes. He didn't quiver in his room all day feeling sorry for himself; he took all those years of repression and fear, all that negative energy, and focused it on creating a new life. He seemed mentally strong and he was determined to succeed.

He'd made it this far after all.

But as the weeks rolled on, the processes and procedures began to chip away at him. The Home Office is an intimidating place for a child. Queuing eight hours just to give a stony-faced official your name and address. Preparing and memorising a witness statement, knowing that every single detail will be cross-examined and scrutinised and if you slip up, you could get sent to the back of the queue. Or back to where you came from.

There were more forms and more queues. More statements and questions. The process went on and on and on and was itself enough to drive anyone mad. But when the whole of your future depended on it, when the decision of these emotionless government officials was literally a matter of life or death for you and when it felt like you had a ticking clock hanging over your head? The anxiety was liable to push you over the edge.

Yonah's decline was rapid. He stopped cooking for the house, then even stopped bothering to cook for himself. He didn't join me to chat over a cup of tea in the morning anymore, he lived on snack foods, barely left his room and his curtains were drawn no matter what time it was.

On the rare occasions I did see him, dragging himself across from the bathroom, his eyes were small and bloodshot, like he'd been crying for days on end.

'You alright, Yonah?' I'd ask.

'Yes, Chris. I am just tired,' he'd say, before disappearing back into the darkness of his room. But I knew it was the Home Office decision he was worried about.

Why was it taking so long?

What more did they need to know?

Will they let me stay? Or will I have to go?

I tried to reassure him, as much as I could.

'It's always like this. You need to put these worries out of your mind,' I said. 'Focus on the things you can control right now, like studying and staying healthy.'

'How can I do that, Chris?' he'd shrug. 'Until I know?'

Then he'd slink away, practically doubled over by the weight of the worries on his slender shoulders. The anxiety was bearing down on him, snuffing out any remaining embers of hope with each passing day.

I began to have serious concerns about his mental health. Every time he vanished into his room a sense of panic would grip my insides until he emerged again, sometimes an hour later, sometimes a day or more. When I was off shift and at home, I'd lay in bed with Androulla sleeping next to me, squeezing my eyes shut and trying to find some respite in sleep but an image kept haunting me.

Breaking into Yonah's room and finding his lifeless body hanging there.

72

I emailed his social worker and told her about how Yonah's behaviour had changed and explained how concerned I was.

'I think we need to try to get him some counselling,' I said in my first email. 'His mental health is in a really bad way. I think he's in an emotionally dangerous place.'

No response.

'I think it would help if he could speak to someone about his anxiety,' I tried, a few days later.

No response.

'Listen, I'm going to be blunt. I'm extremely worried this kid is going to do something stupid, like hang himself,' I said.

I couldn't have been any more clear. I thought that the 17-year-old child whose case she was responsible for – who she had entrusted into our care – was a suicide risk.

I was convinced he was going to kill himself.

But guess what?

Still no response.

Yonah was just another name on her caseload. And he was nearly 18 anyway, so why bother? It was hard enough – and costly enough – to get counselling for British kids, let alone the asylum seekers who were nearly adults in the eyes of the law. I understood the problems of the system only too well. I knew that the chances of getting any support for Yonah in the timeframe we had were slim. But didn't we owe it to him to at least try?

She didn't seem to think so.

In fact, the only contact I had from her and the local authority was a request to move Yonah from my house into accommodation with no support at all. It was a much cheaper option for the remaining months that Yonah would spend in the system. Someone up high had been looking at the balance sheets and spotted an opportunity to save a few quid a month. On paper, Yonah had no special needs; he wasn't ill, he was studying and – well, he was *almost* 18. I assumed they were aware of my concerns but it didn't seem to matter. I don't know how much they would have clawed back – £20, £30, £100?

But Yonah's life was worth more than that to me.

'Absolutely not,' I said. 'The boy needs constant support.'

I dug my heels in and I wouldn't budge. None of us were qualified therapists or mental health practitioners but, in the end, it fell to me and my team to make sure we kept him alive until the decision from the Home Office came in. We watched him like a hawk, while still allowing him his freedom so as not to spook him or cause him to push us away. I introduced him to training and boxing pad work as a way of channelling his fears and anger. When he felt like talking about his past, almost as a form of therapy, I sat with him for hours, listening and asking questions. When he shut down again, we'd take turns to sit with him in silent solidarity.

Then, one day, almost out of the blue, a white envelope with the Home Office stamp came through the letterbox and fluttered down onto the doormat. I picked it up and shouted up the stairs.

'Yonah, I think it's here,' I said.

Yonah tore down the stairs like a whirlwind and grabbed the envelope from me as a couple of other staff members wandered into the hall. It all happened so fast that there wasn't time for us to feel nervous. Yonah had waited long enough and wasn't going to wait a second longer. He tore the envelope open and I held my breath as he pulled out the letter and scanned the small black print on the page.

His smile almost cracked his face in half, stretching right to the top of his ears.

'I can stay!' he said, holding a card that came from the envelope up to my face.

His ARC card. He'd been granted three years' permanent residency.

'Yes!' I yelled, throwing my arms around him. Yonah hugged me back tightly and we stood there for what felt like an eternity. Then I pushed him backwards and clamped my hands to his shoulders.

'This is a lifeline, mate,' I said. 'You know what you need to do now, right?'

'Make my life,' he beamed. 'Tank you, Chris.'

I'd told him a million times over and he'd listened. Once he had that card, he had to go out into the world and make a life for himself. The second that he had the card in his hands, his demeanour changed completely. His eyes lit up and he held his head high.

Within days, he'd worked with his social worker to secure himself somewhere more independent to live, a beautiful self-contained flat with his own bathroom and kitchen in a good area of the city. He enrolled at college so he could learn to be an electrician, bought himself a bike and got a job in the kitchen of a local restaurant.

He went out into the world and he started to make his way.

That little card was all it took to give him back his dignity, hope and life.

The care we provide for children aged 16–18 in the UK, whether they are from here or abroad, should be safe, it should include access to necessary specialist support and it should not discriminate.

But often it fails on all counts.

How could my house ever have been safe for Yonah when the biggest threat he faced was himself and the battles in his own mind? How can we say the system is non-discriminatory when I knew that if the child I requested counselling for was a 16-year-old boy born and raised in London, I'd have stood a much better chance of getting both a reply to my email *and* the support I'd requested?

For the kids within it, the system is segregated in so many ways: by age, by the wealth of the local authority placing them and by the means by which they ended up in care in the first place.

It shouldn't be like this, but it is.

There are many in the UK who believe unaccompanied asylum-seeking children are coming over to this country without good reason to take advantage of our system and leech off the state. They think that a roof over a migrant child's head, £58 per week and legal representation is too much. In reality it is nowhere near enough.

The sad reality for young asylum seekers like Yonah is that they come to England to escape incarceration, famine, murder and rape. The number of applications from unaccompanied asylum-seeking children (UASC) was 3,651 in 2019. A 19 per cent increase compared with 2018.[1] They risk everything and endure so much pain to reach this promised land and the better, safer life it should bring. And what do we do?

We treat them like prisoners.

When they land on our shores, they're essentially taken hostage by the Home Office. Stripped of their rights to even walk outside alone, they await their decision. They are incarcerated by processes and bound by our red tape, their fate in the hands of desk workers who clinically review their paperwork and either approve or deny their application. Office staff who are trained to employ a tick-box approach to human life and decide if they qualify to live or die.

Because that's the reality for many asylum seekers: they go back, they die.

Young people in semi-independent care are already treated like second-class citizens but asylum seekers like Yonah do not

[1] refugeecouncil.org.uk/wp-content/uploads/2020/03/Asylum-Statistics-Annual-Trends-Feb-2020.pdf

even get a class league. They're treated like animals, pushed so far down the bottom of the priority pile that they end up abandoned and forgotten without a second thought as to what impact all that waiting and uncertainty might have on a young mind after a journey that was already filled with horrors we couldn't even begin to imagine. They have a ticking clock hanging over their heads from the moment they arrive here. The Home Office target to make decisions on UK settlement applications is six months but the number of people waiting longer than this has almost doubled in three years. In fact, some people wait years for a decision to be made.[2]

That's a huge problem if you're 17 when you arrive here as things get a lot more difficult as soon as you turn 18. You see, as a minor, the country has a legal obligation to care for you, regardless if you are an asylum seeker, refugee or citizen. Under the age of 18 there is no asylum status granted. As soon as you reach adulthood, you have to *prove* that your life is in danger if you return home *and* that you can stay in this country and not be a nuisance. I have worked with young people who came here as minors and ended up involved in criminal activities, groomed into gangs, who – at 18 – were refused asylum based on basically being vulnerable, abused and manipulated.

Of course there are processes in place. They can appeal against being sent home twice but that just prolongs the pain

---

[2] www.becomecharity.org.uk/care-the-facts/the-big-issues/unaccompanied-asylum-seeking-children/

and anxiety. What's more, after 18 there's no legal aid so how can an asylum seeker with no ARC card and therefore no right to work legally in the UK even think about being able to cover legal costs? It is any wonder many end up working illegally?

Turning 18 is supposed to be a countdown to a landmark age, a milestone. A time to celebrate. Not a slow tick tock, tick tock towards your fate.

It's beyond inhumane.

And do you know what? They think so too, even after all the horrors they have endured.

I have sat with refugees from all corners of the world – young people from Syria and Sudan, from Iraq, Afghanistan and the former Yugoslavia – around kitchen tables and stood with them in snaking Home Office queues and I've seen the agonising process of applying for asylum break them.

'I can't take this. I'd be better going back home.'

Let that sink in.

They believe they would be better going back to poverty, famine, war, imprisonment and the threat of death than stay and be tortured by the inequity and inhumanity of our broken and biased system. Or worse, that they'd rather just end it all.

The prospect of death – by their own hand or their homeland's – is better than living in the hell we've created here.

And those in power still have the audacity to act like saviours? Or suggest that what is given to them is too much?

Like I said, it's beyond inhumane.

CHAPTER FOUR

County Lines

Daniel

IT WAS 2PM WHEN the taxi turned up outside the house. I peered through the window and watched as a tall, thin teenager in a blue tracksuit contorted himself out of the car and threw a grey Nike sports bag over his bony shoulder. It was our newest arrival, fresh out from a stint at Her Majesty's pleasure.

As he pushed the car door shut behind him and paused momentarily, examining every corner of the front of the house, I made my way to the front door to greet him.

'Afternoon, Daniel,' I said, waving.

At first glance, I guessed he was mixed race. I hadn't been told exactly where he was from but you couldn't miss the Mediterranean in him. He was all olive skin and had cheekbones that could cut through glass.

Daniel cocked his head up by way of acknowledgement but he didn't make eye contact.

'Are you Chris?' he asked, staring at his shoes.

As soon as he spoke, I was taken aback. His voice was squeaky, childlike even, and he mumbled like a nervous schoolboy. It was hard to believe he'd just served 12 months for dealing drugs.

'I am indeed,' I said. 'Come on in, mate.'

'Thanks,' he said, finally looking up from the floor.

I felt a familiar pull deep in my chest as my eyes met Daniel's for the first time. This moment was always important to me, every time we got a new resident. They say that the eyes are the windows to the soul but I believe they are a magnifying glass on a person's past too.

Behind Daniel's puppy dog stare all I could see was fear and regret. Big brown eyes full of remorse. This boy might have been gang-affiliated but he was scared too.

'Come in, mate, let's get you sorted out,' I said, putting a hand on his shoulder.

Daniel was an unexpected addition to the house. I'd started my shift that morning with the usual routine – coffee and correspondence. Sitting at my desk, I switched on my computer and opened my emails. A message sent a few minutes earlier, marked with a little red exclamation mark, caught my eye.

EMERGENCY PLACEMENT.

It was from a social worker from the local council called Melissa. She was one of the good ones, out there genuinely trying to make a difference. If she marked something high priority, I knew there'd be a kid in urgent need involved. I clicked on the message and it popped open.

Hi Chris

I have a young person who I need to find a placement for asap.
He's 17 and being released from jail this afternoon. His name
is Daniel, he's quite timid, gang-affiliated but harmless.
    That's all I have.
    Need an answer in the next hour?
    Melissa

Gang-affiliated but harmless? It seemed like a bit of an oxymoron but I trusted Melissa's judgement implicitly, so I started typing my reply.

I spent the morning getting a room ready, putting fresh sheets out and leaving a bottle of water and chocolate bar – bought with my own money as John deemed them 'non-essential' – on the bedside table. Then I made a start on the paperwork. I knew absolutely nothing about Daniel but that was standard.

Sometimes, if you were lucky you got a blurred passport photo so you knew who to look out for but most of the time emergency placements came with no warning or paperwork. Often the most you could hope for was an email with a few details.

Melissa didn't let me down. She sent over everything she had on Daniel. He was from London but because of his gang affiliation, he had to be placed well clear of his 'ends' – the area of the city that was his gang's turf. The city was divided into postcode gangs, where boundary lines were set and had to be respected, if all-out war was to be prevented. You didn't go selling drugs in other gangs' ends – not if you didn't want trouble. Daniel's 'ends' were in north London and he couldn't be placed within ten miles of his home. But it wasn't dealing there or even in other parts of the city that was Daniel's problem. It was being within the clutches of his gang that had landed him in trouble.

You see, Daniel's gang was involved in county lines, where drugs are transported from one area to another, usually across police and local authority boundaries. He wasn't a foot soldier or a fighter, he was a mule, a slave to the commands of gang leaders when orders for drugs came via the 'county line' – the mobile phone line that was used to communicate with buyers from across the county, or 'importing areas' as they are known.

Melissa had made a deal with the Youth Offending Service and the courts for Daniel. He could get early release if he complied with his youth order and stayed away from his old gang life.

Daniel had agreed.

I want to help him break free from that cycle, Melissa wrote.

This boy was still a stranger to me but I wanted the same for him as Melissa did. I believed everyone deserved another chance. My heart was focused on helping a lost young man but a form on my desk reminded me of another obligation.

Pricing.

Usually, emergency placements came to the house through John. By the time I got the details, he'd have totted up the cost to us, added on the mark-up and done the negotiation. A young person with a history like Daniel warranted a high price, especially when the placement meant they could be released from juvenile detention into safety imminently. There were other factors too, like which local authority they were coming from. But it was the damage and risk that mattered the most.

In this sector, the most broken things are the most valuable.

An average resident would need between six and eight hours of key work per week but Daniel needed more. Much more. In the end, I worked out he needed about 14 hours a week, costing the authorities about £2,000 per week, although John picked up negotiations once he got wind of the placement so I never found out the exact figure. By the time everything was sorted, signed and filed, five hours had passed and that's when I heard the brakes of Daniel's taxi pulling up outside.

I couldn't show it but I hated the process of getting people settled into the house; it was always heart-breaking. Every single time. Imagine being 17 years old and turning up at a strange house in an unfamiliar area, carrying your worldly possessions in one small bag and the weight of your secrets on your shoulders. They had no one by their side for that bit of moral support and no idea what they were walking into. They just had to take whatever was available. After all, anything was better than jail, wasn't it?

Unfortunately that wasn't always the case.

Not every house was clean, relaxed and safe, like mine. Not every house manager believed in giving everyone a fresh start in life. The thought of where they might have ended up would always play on my mind and I'd have to snap myself back to the fact they'd turned up on MY doorstep.

Sitting at the kitchen table, I noticed how Daniel's demeanour seemed directly at odds with his appearance. He might have been slight but he looked tough. His hair was cropped military short and he had a distinctive tattoo on the nape of his neck. It reminded me of one of David Beckham's tattoos, angel wings of some kind with the initials 'A. J.' beneath it. He looked tough alright but he was hunched over in his seat, like he was trying to make himself smaller, invisible even.

It turned out that 'A.J.' were the initials of his best friend who'd died in a car accident when he was 12. He'd needed counselling at the time but Melissa told me that he'd never really gotten over it.

'Talking about it will trigger his depression,' she warned.

'If he wants to talk to me about it, I'll be all ears,' I said. 'But if not, I won't bring it up.'

When dealing with personal trauma, I always left it in the young person's hands. I never forced uncomfortable conversations because I knew from my own experiences they could do more harm than good.

He was looking down at his hands again as I started to speak.

'I want to make something clear. I don't care what you've done in the past,' I said. 'The moment you walked through these doors you got a clean slate, do you understand?'

I said it to all of the boys who came to us and I always meant it. I wasn't always sure if they *wanted* the clean slate they were being offered but I sensed that Daniel did. He looked at me sideways as I said it, eyes feeling me out and analysing if he could trust me.

'I will respect you like I respect everyone else in the house,' I continued. 'I only ask for one thing.'

'Yeah, what's that?' Daniel asked.

'You treat me with the same reverence,' I said.

'Reverence?' he frowned. 'What's that?'

'It's respect, but deeper,' I said.

A smile crept across his lips.

'I like that word,' he said.

And just like that, the ice was broken. I showed Daniel to his room and left him to get his things unpacked while I went back to my office to print off our policy guidelines for new residents.

We did our best to be as relaxed as possible but we had to have rules in place for insurance purposes. We might be an unregulated provision but we had standards and processes to keep us all safe. Once he'd unpacked, Daniel came to my office and tapped gingerly on the door.

'Come in, mate, and sit down while I go through the house rules,' I said, gesturing towards the empty chair opposite me. 'Save any questions for the end.'

'OK,' he mumbled, sitting down.

I rattled through the list.

'Respect the house rules and bear in mind other young people live here too. So, if you cook then make sure you clean up after yourself. You'll get £58 a week to live on. We don't keep money here so please don't ask us for it. If you find yourself short of anything essential – food or toiletries, for example – don't do anything silly. Speak to me first and I will sort something out.'

He nodded and I continued.

'No outside friends allowed in your bedroom. No girlfriends or partners in your bedroom. I say this to everyone, that's to protect you in case someone makes an accusation. Do you understand?'

He nodded.

'No drugs or alcohol. No knives, no guns – you can see where I am going with this, yeah?' I said.

He nodded again but with his background I needed more.

'Daniel, look at me,' I said. 'No drugs or alcohol. No knives, no guns. OK?'

'Yeah, of course,' he said.

'Good,' I replied.

'Now, what else . . . ' I paused, looking down at the sheet of paper on my desk. 'Oh, yes, that's it. Keep your room clean and tidy,' I added. 'Do you have any questions?'

'What happens with money when I turn 18?' he asked.

'Everything is covered by the local authorities until you are 18. After that we'll sign you up to universal credit and housing.'

I looked at the paperwork, then looked up. 'It's your birthday in a few weeks, isn't it?'

'Yeah,' he said.

'OK, well, you don't need to worry about that just yet. We'll be there to help you with it when the time comes,' I said. 'Anything else?'

Daniel shook his head.

'Right, I think that's it. My office is the only place that is out of bounds. This is your home now. I'm here to support you where I can, as are the rest of the team, who you'll meet later,' I said. 'I can be your friend or just another annoying professional, that's entirely up to you. I like to be both.'

Daniel laughed.

'If I'm in here though, my door is always open, just knock first,' I added.

'Reverence,' Daniel smiled, raising an eyebrow.

'Yes, mate,' I grinned. 'Welcome to the team.'

It was how I always finished my rules and policy chat. I wanted the boys to know they were part of something here. A team that worked together. That looked out for one another.

'Cup of tea?' I said, standing up from my chair.

Formalities out of the way, I now needed to try and get to know the lad, to make him feel welcome and safe.

'Yes please, two sugars,' he replied.

As the days passed, Daniel relaxed into life in the house. Well, as much as he could. But there was always a darkness behind his brown eyes. The shadow of his gang life lingered behind him, the tentacles of the past stretching towards him, threatening to tighten around him and pull him back.

He was a young man trapped between his past and future.

We'd sit together in the kitchen, me with a coffee, Daniel with a sugary tea, and he'd open up to me about his life with the gang.

'The gang always came first,' he said. 'And I was at the very bottom of the pecking order. I had no choice but to do what I was told.'

The gang owned him and he worked for the gang.

His shift started on a Thursday.

'There was no rota or schedule. They just gave you a £10 burner phone – a cheap one you could just throw away – and when the call came you just had to get ready and wait to be picked up, wherever you were.'

'Did you know where you were going?' I asked.

'Never. No direction. No knowledge. Nothing,' he said. 'Once, in the early days I asked.'

'What did they say?' I asked.

'Shut the fuck up and wait until you get there. Some days the landscape was rolling green hills, other times we'd be by the sea. I'd stare out of the car window, watching the waves crashing against the rocks.'

'What happened when you got to wherever you were going?' I asked.

'That was when the work started. I never knew where they were going to leave me. I could be in a council estate in the north of England somewhere or a fucking field in the Midlands. They'd dump me with some of their stuff and tell me where to deliver by text or phone call. It was relentless. I didn't sleep or shower for three days. Sometimes I didn't even eat or drink on a shift.'

'Nothing at all?' I gasped.

'Just the cocaine,' he said. 'That's all they'd let me have. It was the only thing that kept me going. "You can eat on Sunday" – that's what they'd tell me. The days would blur, sometimes I'd be so tired I wanted to collapse but I knew I couldn't.'

A wave of sadness washed over me.

How the hell had he survived all that?

'The worst jobs were to the houses in the middle of nowhere. The ones the gangs there had taken over.'

Cuckooing, I thought. It is a common tactic used by county lines gangs. Local drug dealers take over the home of a vulnerable person and use it as a base for trafficking.

'Those were always owned by dirty old men. Perverts. Or smackheads. I hated them,' he said, physically recoiling from the memory. 'But the whole thing, it was just relentless. Your phone would buzz and buzz and buzz,' he said. 'You'd deliver hundreds of wraps. Hundreds. It felt like it would never end. Then eventually, you'd get the message. "Outside." The car would be there, waiting. You never talked about what happened. You just got in and kept your mouth shut.'

He fell silent and stared into his mug, swirling the undissolved sugar granules around in the beige liquid. Then he looked up at me. For a moment, his eyes were bright and childlike.

'I used to play a game with myself on the way home, Chris. First one to spot Canary Wharf wins,' he said. 'I never lost.'

I laughed affectionately at the pride he exuded in this statement.

'So what happened when you got home?' I asked.

'They just kicked you out of the car, gave you your pocket money and gave you your orders,' he shrugged.

'Which were?' I asked.

'Don't get arrested, don't go missing. We'll be back for you next week,' he said.

For his time and work, Daniel would be paid £20.

Back in north London, Daniel lived with his gran on a council estate with some notoriety for being rough. When he returned home on a Sunday night, he told me that she would always make him take his clothes off at the door.

'I didn't blame her. I'd practically crawl in,' he said. 'And I stank – of sweat, damp, mouldy drug houses and God knows what else. I wouldn't have so much as washed my hands for days.'

As he described the state he'd return home in, I gagged. I knew what teenage boys smelled like at the best of times but what Daniel described was something else. The smell of dirt and despair.

'It was horrible,' he said. 'But that was what made it so good to be home.'

Daniel would use his 'pocket money' from the gang to order a large pizza before jumping in the bath. After eating, he'd go to bed, barely able to keep his eyes open. He'd sleep until Monday afternoon. On Tuesdays, he spent time with his gran, the woman who had raised him from birth. His mum had left before he'd even had time to learn how to nestle into her chest as he slept. She only loved drugs and the latest man on the scene. Raising a child just didn't fit in.

But Daniel's gran opened her arms and her home.

'I don't really remember my mum. She died when I was young,' he explained. 'So it was just me and my gran. She knows everyone on our estate. People respected her because she'd been around so long.'

She might have come before the gangs and she might have earned their respect because she was a God-fearing woman who was friends with all of *their* grandparents. But even that couldn't save Daniel from his fate. It was do or die on those estates. As soon as a boy hit puberty, he had to contribute – or pay the price.

'They'd speak so nicely to my gran. They'd sit and drink tea with her,' he said. 'But once I was alone with them, they'd threaten me. Say if I didn't do as I was told, they'd hurt her. What was I supposed to do? We only had each other.'

Tuesdays were their special day.

'It was my favourite day of the week. We'd just curl up together on the sofa and watch TV all day.'

Then he looked directly at me.

'I love *The Chase*,' he told me excitedly. 'I could take on The Beast any day, honestly.'

My heart ached. That was it. That was his window of normality. Less than 48 hours where he got to be a child, enjoying the things that normal teenagers did – junk food, family time and crap TV.

But he couldn't switch off. Not for long. Because as soon as Wednesday rolled round, he had to prepare for his next shift.

'I ate as much as I could. Gran cooked lots of traditional dishes. Meat and potatoes, fish. I ate those and anything else I could get my hands on. Crisps and stuff like that. And I slept too,' he said. 'I had to store up my energy.'

It was the only thing he could control. The gang would come, no matter what. He couldn't run or hide. They'd find him. All he could do was prepare to survive another shift. Week in, week out, it was the same routine.

'Did your gran know where you were going?' I asked.

Daniel shrugged. 'She didn't ask many questions. I told her I was staying with friends over the weekend and she said she believed me,' he said. 'But I don't think she did, really. She knew I was involved in *something* bad, she just expected God to sort it all out. She talked about him a lot, telling me that if I smoked drugs I'd be rejected at the gates of heaven. That I wasn't bad, I just hadn't found God yet. That was her way of trying to help. She was convinced He'd protect me but it never felt like that.'

There was no let-up, no annual leave for Daniel. This wasn't a job, it was a hostage situation. And if mistakes were made, there was a price to pay.

'One night, I was so tired that I fell asleep and missed calls. Not just one or two, hundreds of them,' he said. 'It was like my body had just given in. One moment I was sat down, just taking the weight off my feet. The next I was awake, lying in a pool of my own blood with fists flying into my face and head.'

When they hadn't been able to reach him and deliveries weren't made, they'd tracked him down and found him asleep. They'd woken him by raining blows down on him. That was the price you paid when you cost the gang money.

'My face was shattered but I was still expected to finish my shift,' he said. 'I couldn't even look at Gran when I got home that Sunday. I didn't want her to worry.'

After that, Daniel lived in fear.

'The drugs they gave me to stay awake, the speed and the coke, they made me sick and gave me severe diarrhoea but I was too scared to go to the toilet in case I missed a drop,' he said. 'So I just shat my pants.'

No matter how hard he tried to do what he was told, the exhaustion meant mistakes were inevitable.

'I was doing a drop. I'd been going for three days. The coke was wearing off and my eyelids were down to my knees,' he recalled. 'I could barely stand up so it was no surprise I missed the signs.'

He didn't even see the flashing blue lights spinning towards him in the early hours of the morning in the nondescript suburban town he'd been transported to. His pockets were bulging with supplies so there'd be no pleading personal use. Daniel was well and truly busted. He was arrested and sent to a juvenile detention centre for three months before he was released.

'I didn't want to leave,' he said. 'I was scared. I knew I was going to pay for my mistake, I just didn't know how.'

He was released on a Tuesday. On Thursday, a car pulled up outside his gran's. He was given a new phone and the routine started again. Only now, there was a debt to pay. There'd be no pocket money for his large pizza after this shift. Now he had to work for free. Once you were in debt to the gang, there was no getting out.

'I just had to be thankful they didn't do something worse,' he said.

But it wasn't long before Daniel made his next mistake. He was making a delivery to a house in Wales when it was raided by the police. This time he was sent down for six months.

'I knew I'd never be able to go home after that,' he said. 'I knew the gang would kill me, one way or the other.'

By putting a gun to his head or working him to death.

As his release date crept closer, the fear built in Daniel.

'People say anything's better than jail, Chris, but you're wrong,' he said. 'It was a safe haven for me. Away from the gang, three meals a day and a bed to sleep in.'

I felt my cheeks redden as I remembered what I'd thought on the day Daniel moved in: *Anything's better than jail, right?*

But I wasn't right. He was. I'd been naïve to think that what awaited lads like Daniel when they got out was better than being inside. They were living a hell on earth, barely visible to most of us.

'I threatened to kill myself if they were going to release me,' he said. 'It was the only way I could see to escape.'

'Well, you're safe now,' I said. 'No one is coming to get you here. That's why we have strict rules and boundaries. It's not to stop you from going out, it's to stop bad company from getting in.'

'I hope so,' he said, his voice barely a whisper.

I genuinely believed that we could protect Daniel. All the necessary safeguarding was in place and he was miles away from his ends. He wasn't interested in going out and getting into trouble so we didn't have to worry about him like we did some of the other residents. He was content just having the chance to live like a child for the first time in years.

Maurine, an older member of my team, took him under her wing. I often thought she mothered him a bit too much but, after everything he'd been through, I felt like he needed that bit of care and tenderness. Maurine had it in spades.

We did everything we could to keep him occupied, to turn his mind from the past that kept him trapped and threatened his entire future. We watched as he embraced hobbies long left behind, like music, writing lyrics and tinkering with motorbikes. He even started looking at college courses in mechanical engineering. There were activities and keywork sessions like cooking, art classes that allowed him to express his hopes and fears and weight training, to help him build up his strength and focus his mind.

Oh, and the TV too. Daniel loved the TV.

Or maybe it was what it represented?

Like Daniel relaxed into those hours with his gran, you could see him practically melt into the couch when we gathered to watch movies together as a team, a house. That was something he'd never felt before. It was different again to just being him and his gran. With me and Maurine and the other boys in the house, we were a unit.

A family.

The darkness behind Daniel's eyes began to shift and you could tell he was beginning to see a different future for himself.

He said as much to me one night after I flicked off the TV and ushered the boys to their rooms.

Daniel was about to walk through the doorway when he stopped suddenly and turned to look at me.

'Thanks for everything, Chris,' he said. 'I really feel like there's a chance things will be OK. You know?'

'They will, mate,' I smiled. 'Goodnight.'

I knew something wasn't right as soon as I stepped into the house to start my shift. The house felt empty, incomplete. I hastily made my way to the office. The door was open and Maurine was sitting there with sadness etched across her face.

My stomach sank into my shoes. I knew that look.

Something's happened to one of the boys.

'What is it?' I asked, not even bothering to take my coat off.

'It's Daniel,' Maurine said. 'He's gone.'

The room suddenly started to spin around me. Daniel didn't ever leave the house without us because he was too scared to. He lived in fear of seeing a member of his old gang and being dragged back into that life. If he was gone, it was because they had found him.

We pieced together his movements. The staff on the night shift didn't see or hear anything out of the ordinary. Daniel was his usual, pleasant self. He'd made himself some dinner at about 7pm, watched a little TV and chatted with some of the other boys. At 10pm he went to his room, like he usually did. He didn't emerge from his room the following morning when the other boys did, but then that wasn't unusual, he'd been known to spend full days in bed, so the staff on duty didn't think much of it.

But when Maurine started her shift at 9pm the next evening and did her rounds to say hello to everyone, she found Daniel's room empty.

'We've checked every room in the house but he was nowhere,' she said, shaking her head sadly.

'Let's check the security cameras,' I said.

Scanning through the grainy footage from the four cameras in the house, we followed Daniel's movements. From 10pm there was nothing but stillness. Then, at somewhere between 5am and 6am, the camera that was trained on the front door sprang to life. The door inched open and a figure emerged from the house. A skinny, hunched-over figure with a grey Nike bag slung over his shoulder.

It was unmistakably Daniel. He pulled the hood of his blue tracksuit up around his razor-sharp cheekbones, put his head down and walked away.

It was the last time I ever saw him.

We did everything we could to bring him back. I called the police to report him missing.

'I'd like to report a missing child – a boy called Daniel,' I said. 'I'm the manager of the semi-independent accommodation he lives in.'

'Age?' the officer asked.

'Seventeen,' I said.

'When was he last seen?' the officer asked.

'This morning between 5am and 6am,' I said. 'We saw him leaving the house on the security camera.'

'He's only been gone a few hours,' the officer queried. 'Does he have a habit of going missing?'

'No. He is gang affiliated and has been involved in county lines,' I explained. 'But he moved away from that life. We're concerned his old gang may have found him and coerced him back.'

Even down the telephone line I could feel the officer's interest dissolve at the mention of county lines.

'Oh, they normally go back to old ways after a while,' he said. 'I'm sure he'll pop up in a police station soon.'

I clenched my fists. *Or maybe a morgue, you fucking moron*, I thought.

'Officer, this boy had made excellent progress. We are quite sure that if he's gone, it's not been a free choice. Will you be able to go out and look for him?' I said, fighting to keep my tone balanced, when all I wanted to do was scream.

Do your fucking job and look for him.

'I'll ask our squads to keep an eye out,' he said. 'But we are very busy at the moment.'

Daniel's life meant nothing to them. Branded a county lines kid, he lost any value in their eyes. I couldn't help but wonder if their attitude would have been different if they looked past his label to see the boy I'd come to know.

But they were probably too busy for that.

After I hung up from the police, I tried to call Melissa but she didn't answer so I wrote her an email. She needed to know as soon as possible and I didn't want her hearing it from anyone else.

Hi Melissa.

I have some bad news. Daniel was seen leaving the placement at 5am this morning with his bag. I have reported it to the police but I am not holding my breath. I am gutted as the team was making great progress with him. He was even looking at starting a college course.

I will keep you posted if I hear anything.

Chris Wild

A few hours later, Melissa emailed back.

Hi Chris

You did your best. Six weeks was more than we expected.

Let's see if he turns up.

Keep me posted.

Thank you.

Melissa

Daniel was weeks from turning 18 when he came to the house. We had the smallest of windows to help him turn his life around and get him back into a normal routine. Honestly, I felt like we were almost there, like we'd helped him break the chains that bound him to the gang. I was heartbroken when he vanished. I couldn't help but wonder if we'd missed something, if there was something more we could have done. But that's how these gangs operate: by preying on the most vulnerable children, exploiting their fears and weaknesses and using them for their own commercial gain.

Daniel's fate was out of our hands now, not just because he was out of the house but because he would turn 18 in a matter of days. An adult in the eyes of the law. The next time he made a mistake he'd find himself in a different jail than he'd known before, with bigger and scarier criminals. I wondered if it would still feel like his safe haven or if he'd just spin through his life alternating between two versions of hell.

It was two weeks before we had any news. Then, one day, Melissa called.

'The police cracked down on two major London gangs running county lines out of the city,' Melissa said. 'One of them was Daniel's.'

'Was he with them?' I asked, my heart in my throat.

'Yes, he was arrested in one of the raids,' Melissa said.

I almost choked on the conflicting emotions. First, the relief that he was alive. After everything he'd told me, I couldn't assume that he was well. But if he was still breathing, he still had a chance . . . Then my heart sank. He'd get proper time for this. Three, maybe four years. The courts wouldn't come to us looking for a character reference. He'd be sent down without question. By the time he got out, he'd be into his twenties and the support we had been able to offer him this time would no longer be available to him. Despite his vulnerability, despite everything, he'd be completely on his own. The world would consider him independently responsible for his own actions, ignoring the bind the gang held him in. The one he'd never be able to escape.

The county lines trade has exploded in recent years. In 2018, the National Crime Agency (NCA) reported that there were 2,000 individual deal lines in the UK, linked to 1,000 branded county lines.[1] Each one was capable of making up to £5,000 per day. The people running these operations, the 'kingpins' sending out the orders as they flash their ill-gotten gains on social media, are recruiting directly from the care system to maintain their dirty business. In January 2019, the National Police Chiefs' Council (NPCC) said that about 10,000 children, some as young as ten years old, were being criminally exploited.[2] Kids like Daniel.

County lines is a modern-day iteration of Fagin's gang in *Oliver Twist*. It's a form of modern slavery, no different to child labour of days gone by, where young people were forced

---

[1] www.nationalcrimeagency.gov.uk/who-we-are/publications/257-county-lines-drug-supply-vulnerability-and-harm-2018/file

[2] www.bbc.co.uk/news/av/uk-49389392

to work in cotton mills in arduous conditions. The poorest and most vulnerable of society being used to do the dirty work for rich criminals pulling all the strings. They might not have to scramble into machinery to unthread a piece of cotton that's stopping mass production but being involved with county lines is just as dangerous and, tragically, the lives of those ensnared in it are just as short.

Children in care are vulnerable, desperate to fit in or too scared to defy orders that come from people they believe have the power to harm them. Cash-strapped councils in urban areas struggle to find affordable houses or foster homes locally for older children so they send them to privately run provisions in cheaper rural and suburban areas miles away from any friends or family. Once they leave the care sector and come into semi-independent or supported accommodation, they're even more exposed than they were before. It only takes one bad placement, with staff members who don't care, or being forced to stay in a hostel full of criminals and drug users because there's nowhere else to go, for a child to slip through the net into a life of pain, violence and trauma with these drug gangs. We fail them time and time again.

In December 2019, a BBC report revealed that about 30,000 children in care lived outside of their local area, with nearly 12,000 placed 20 miles from their homes.[3] In the context of county lines, this can have an enormous impact – it essentially creates a brand new 'line' for criminal gangs.

---

[3] www.bbc.co.uk/news/uk-50899652

Miles from anything they know, isolated, scared and alone, these children begin to spiral and the leaders of these gangs know exactly where to find them, in those unassuming houses tucked away in residential streets. They befriend them, gain their trust and once they have it, they abuse them.

Even when attempts are made to help kids out of county lines, the system falls short. Like the 15-year-old kid who was moved 100 miles away from his home to the South East to avoid his past life. His new local authority refused to pick his case up as he already had a social worker in his home authority. His old social worker refused to commit to the 100-mile commute to visit him, so he was left with no one.[4] He was identified as a child in need and yet no one stepped up to help him.

In the end he was stabbed in the street.

The more I see it happening, the more I see the parallels between the story of *Oliver Twist* and county lines gangs. County lines are glorified in music, TV and on social media. It's made to look appealing to disenfranchised youths. As a seven-year-old, I watched *Oliver!*, with the singing and dancing, and I was enthralled. I couldn't wait to grow up, be a thief and have lots of fun . . . and money!

As fate would have it, I ended up in care and did end up in a gang. I was 11 years old when I took my first beating from an older boy. I'd been keeping watch while he broke into someone's house but I missed the owners coming back home.

---

[4] www.bbc.co.uk/news/uk-england-54570803

I panicked and ran without warning him. He managed to escape but my actions weren't forgotten. Back on our estate, he found me, punched me full force in the face, told me I had cost him nearly £500 and I had to make it back. I was in debt to the gang and I'd never been so scared. For the next six months, I did whatever he told me to do – delivering packages, keeping watch, shoplifting. None of it was fun. Not so *Oliver!* after all.

The same is true today. There's nothing glamorous about being in a county line. I've never met a single young person who's told me it was amazing and that they made loads of money. Someone is making an abundance of cash alright but they're the ones staying well clear of the limelight. The police and local authorities don't even know who these people are, no one ever does. It's like the Banksy effect: we know they exist, we even know who they *might* be, but unless they're caught red-handed we'll never know.

A few months after Daniel vanished, a police officer told me that every time they raided a county line drug den the young people never ran away. They just stood there.

'Some of them even begged to be locked up,' he said.

Daniel immediately sprang to my mind. The tales of everything he'd been through. And he was just one of thousands like him. Treated like slaves, abused, beaten, threatened, starved, deprived of sleep, deprived of sunlight, deprived of any chance to ever leave that life.

Prison was an escape.

This is the harsh reality of young people caught up in county lines. It's not some glittering criminal lifestyle they've chosen, like it's portrayed in TV programmes like *Top Boy* or the movie *Blue Story*, which glamorise gang life and county lines, making it look like an aspirational career choice.

In 2020, at the start of the first national lockdown, I went on BBC Radio 5 to talk about county lines and why so many young people from the care sector go missing. It made me think about Daniel's plight. While we never learned exactly what – or who – prompted him to get up and leave the house that morning, we have a pretty good idea. His gang needed him back on that line to keep the drugs getting to where they needed to be.

The question shouldn't really be why so many kids go missing, it should be what's driving this machine that keeps enslaving them. As the radio discussion circled, I came to my point: it's not the gangs themselves, it's the demand for drugs.

'It's an economy inside an economy,' I said. 'When rich people stop taking drugs, then children will stop going missing and killing each other.'

I stand by that statement. As long as the rich want illegal drugs, there will be criminal gangs – not just here but across the globe – that will exploit that demand and our poorest and most damaged children will always be the ones who supply it.

CHAPTER FIVE
Recruitment

Ifaz

I SAT BOLT UPRIGHT in my pull-out bed, jerked out of a deep slumber. Something had given me such a shock that my heart was thumping against my chest so hard that I could hear it reverberating around the walls of the house.

BANG. BANG. BANG.

I rubbed my eyes as I tried to figure out what it was that had disturbed me.

BANG. BANG. BANG.

Suddenly I realised. My heart *was* pounding but the noise I could hear wasn't that. It was the sound of someone hammering on the front door. I looked at my clock. Midnight.

My stomach churned. A knock that vigorous at this time could only mean one of two things: a visit from the police to arrest someone or a visit from someone altogether more undesirable. Either way, it was trouble for me and trouble for the boys. Adrenaline kicked in as I quickly pulled on my clothes and shoes.

I darted to the stairs, then hesitated. There were no blue lights flashing and no shadows of uniformed figures stretching through the windows. This wasn't the police. So who was it?

BANG. BANG. BANG.

I was launched back into action by the sound. I slipped into the office and tried to catch a glimpse through the camera over the front door. I could see someone in the doorway but they were being deliberately evasive, pulling up their hood and walking away from the camera after every series of knocks.

I considered the possible scenarios. It could be a new arrival that I'd not been made aware of but that was unlikely. The person could simply have the wrong address . . .

Or this could be a set-up.

There were gang-affiliated boys in the house and it wasn't unusual for rival gangs to try to get inside to exact revenge for one thing or another. As house manager, it was a risk of the job and it was my call to decide whether I answered it or not. I rubbed my chin. Maybe if I ignored them, they'd just go away?

BANG. BANG. BANG.

'Or not,' I said out loud.

There was only one thing for it. I took to my feet, walked to the front door and opened it a crack.

'Yes?' I said abruptly.

My foot was jammed behind the door frame in case any-one tried to force their way in. The figure spun around, pulled down his hood and looked at me.

'Is this the hostel?' he asked, in a London street accent.

He was tiny and looked like a little mouse. Specifically, like Fievel from *An American Tail*, all swallowed up in his massive black coat. I'd have laughed if I hadn't been on such high alert. He might've appeared harmless but I'd worked the job long enough to know not to take anything for granted or take unnecessary risks. Gangs didn't send thugs to go knocking on the doors of professionally-run care homes. They used people who looked innocent, like butter wouldn't melt, so you'd drop your guard.

'The what, mate?' I said.

No one called them hostels anymore. That was a throwback to my own time in care, decades earlier.

'The hostel,' he repeated.

'No,' I said. I was about to shut the door, then suddenly a thought flashed through my mind. A phone call I'd had with the company director, Cesar, earlier in the week.

'We might have a new arrival this week. A Middle Eastern boy. I'll let you know if it goes through . . .'

He never had. But glancing back at the confused-looking boy on my doorstep, I wondered. *Is he Middle Eastern? Had Cesar mentioned anything else about him . . . ?*

Then I remembered.

'Are you from Wembley by any chance?' I asked cautiously. Cesar had said that the potential new arrival was from that end of the city, so it was worth a try.

'Yes, mate. Are you Chris?' he replied with a smile.

I heaved a sigh of relief and opened the door fully.

'Yes, I am,' I said. 'Come on in. What's your name again?'

'Ifaz,' he said.

'Nice to meet you Ifaz,' I said. 'I'm sorry, I wasn't expecting you at this time.'

I was pissed off at Cesar. And I was pissed off at whoever Ifaz's social worker was, too. This kind of thing was becoming a regular occurrence – Cesar agreeing a placement and not telling me about it and social workers not even bothering to escort the kids in their care to their new home. I was furious that this young boy was at my door late at night, on his own and without his social worker. Ifaz couldn't have been more than 16 years old and was carrying a plastic bag containing his worldly belongings – a few tracksuit bottoms and a baseball cap. Would they be happy if their own teenage child was walking the streets of London in the middle of the night like this? I doubted it. They were professionals with a legal duty of care to serve and protect, not to mention being human beings who should have more compassion for these young people.

How did they sleep at night?

I made Ifaz a cup of tea and invited him to sit at the kitchen table.

'Here,' I said. 'Have that while I sort out your room.'

I'd tried to call Cesar to get more information but he was drunk in a fancy wine bar somewhere, slurring and laughing. I'd have to wait until the morning when he'd sobered up to get any sense out of him.

A little detective work allowed me to piece together just enough about Ifaz to be able to get him settled in the house. Turned out, he'd been living on the streets for the past few days waiting for his social worker to find him some alternative accommodation after he'd got himself in trouble with a local gang member. He'd needed to leave his previous placement immediately for his own safety.

It was 1am before I got back into bed. I'd put Ifaz in our last available room and explained that we'd go through all the paperwork the next day.

'You just get a good night's sleep for now,' I'd said.

'Thanks, Chris,' he'd replied.

I barely slept a wink, I was so vexed. Anger generated kinetic energy in my body that caused me to toss and turn. In the end, at about 5am, I gave up and decided to get up and get to work. Cleaning the kitchen area and mopping the floor was always my first task of the day, followed by tidying the living area and making sure the front and back gardens were neat and safe.

It was a habit I inherited from my father. He'd get up early every day to clean the house from top to bottom before work. He always said it was his first achievement of the day.

Wake up. Make your bed. Clean the house. Feel proud.

I carried that ethos wherever I worked. In the children's homes and now here in semi-independent provisions, it was a gift I gave to the kids I was responsible for. I never wanted them to wake up to a dirty house.

A clean house is a safe house. A safe house is a home.

Today, after the unsettling arrival he'd experienced, I was particularly keen to make Ifaz feel welcome. Once the cleaning was done, I set about contacting the relevant authorities to find out exactly who he was. He'd been reluctant to tell me much when we'd chatted briefly over a brew the night before, which wasn't unusual. Most young people in the care sector are guarded and nervous around people in authority. It's a form of self-preservation. Their trust has to be earned.

A few hours later, his local authority responded and I scheduled a placement meeting for later in the week before settling down to read the stack of paperwork they'd sent to me. I understood trauma. I'd lived it myself and seen it in the young people I'd cared for. But Ifaz's story was a world apart.

He'd been born into a war zone. Where most children begin life with love, safety and security, his began surrounded by fear, pain and death. Trauma was one of his first experiences. His homeland was divided and innocent children like him were considered collateral damage as warring factions rained shells and shrapnel down on their homes. Soon there was nothing left. No swings and roundabout to play on, just the crumbling remains of their neighbours' homes, dusted with broken glass and fragments of shattered lives.

His referral form read like the screenplay for a Hollywood war film. The detail was so painful and gruesome that I had to take breaks to allow myself time to comprehend what I was reading. Ifaz was only young when he came to England with his family to escape the war. At first, his memories were a blur to him but as he grew up, they crept back into his consciousness.

'Ifaz began suffering flashback nightmares of decapitated heads and bullets being fired at buildings as a teenager,' the report read.

My heart ached to think what this tiny, wide-eyed child had seen. The memories he lived with and how they must still impact him now.

'In his home country, anyone who left a light on was a target for enemy soldiers. This is a memory that has haunted Ifaz and when he first settled in a safe house in England he slept with his light on every night as an act of defiance,' the report continued. It was a useful thing to know and it suggested a certain fighting spirit too.

Ifaz went to school and managed to get himself an education. He and his family were eventually awarded permanent residency so they'd never be sent back to the country they'd fled. His parents worked hard in low-paid jobs to feed and care for Ifaz and his sister. But they didn't quite have the Hollywood movie happy-ever-after.

Ifaz was put through a trauma framework that was intended to reintegrate survivors into loving and supportive environments, accelerate the brain's healing process, untangle the nervous system from the immobility response, eliminate sources of re-traumatisation and help him adapt to the potential for a positive future.

But things didn't quite work that way for Ifaz.

There are those who are fortunate enough to grow up in London's neighbourhoods, who attend good schools that enable them to flourish and succeed. Then there are those who don't. The poor and disadvantaged who can't afford the price of security, whose histories write their future and whose only aspiration can be survival.

People like Ifaz.

In order to survive, he gravitated towards bad company. The company of criminal gangs who introduced him to a world of precarious opportunity. His affiliation was defined by the post-code within which his parents had settled. But the streets of London didn't suggest danger to him. The chances of getting shot here were low in comparison to the places he'd played as a child. After years of being surrounded by death and destruction, he feared nothing and his fearlessness became a badge of honour among his peers – his education a hidden weapon. He earned the respect of his people, attracted the attention of gang leaders and before long, he was leading a crew of his own.

Which is how he'd ended up on my doorstep.

A postcode war had broken out. A conflict between gangs over territory defined by the city's postcode areas. More often than not it started with media intimidation – music videos displaying the power and wealth of one gang and denigrating rival neighbourhood. It always ended in violence or death.

Despite being just 16 years old and barely touching five foot four, Ifaz's rapid ascension through the ranks made him a target. Not that it fazed him. He moved because it was smart, not because he was scared. Being chased by young people on bikes with knives did not frighten him, not after he'd dodged bullets in a war zone on a daily basis. That's what had put him at the front of the queue when it came to recruitment.

Ifaz didn't let me see that part of him though, not at first. In the house, he was calm, kind and observant. Like a professional poker player, he watched everyone around him, never showing his cards. Despite the fact he dressed and spoke 'street', in conversation he came across as kind and considerate, a young man who loved and lived for his mum, dad and younger sister. His parents had done all they could to keep him on the right path. But Ifaz saw the injustice of their situation, as they slaved away working two jobs each on less than minimum wage just to keep a roof over the family's head and food on the table.

'Why don't you try and do things the right way?' I'd say. 'You're bright, you're educated. You can do more than this.'

'In this country?' he scoffed. 'I'm not going to be a donkey like my parents.'

'What do you mean?' I asked.

'They can only get the work no one from this country wants,' he said. 'Cleaning, building, hard physical work that your people leave for people like me.'

He meant asylum seekers.

'When my family came to London we lived in a box room in a shared house. I could hear my parents crying at night because they didn't have enough money to feed everyone,' he said, anger creasing his young face. 'My dad would go for days without food just so me and my sister could eat. That was no life.'

I nodded as Ifaz explained how a rogue landlord had crammed 20 people like sardines into a five-bedroom semi-detached house. All of them were people who had risked their lives to escape war and devastation in foreign lands and find a new and better life in England.

'They were all disappointed,' Ifaz spat. 'They were treated like animals. We all were.'

What could I say? How was I meant to convince a young man to keep on the straight and narrow when he'd seen people he cared for abused by so-called 'legitimate' businessmen, who bent and reshaped the rules and took advantage of these people's vulnerable status, just so they could make a pretty profit? All Ifaz was doing was refusing to become a victim of that repression the only way he knew how.

Months passed and I worked closely with Ifaz, trying to help him see sense. I pushed him towards further education, time and again. For a while, it felt like I might be getting through to him but then the cracks in his 'good boy' façade started to show. He started flashing cash around the house that definitely hadn't come from saving his weekly allowance. Not literally, mind. Ifaz was smarter than that. He used his comparative wealth to splash out on Nando's and Pizza Hut when most of the boys were living on dry bread and Super Noodles. When he ordered in, the other boys circled around him like pigeons, all bobbing and bowing in the hope of picking up a scrap.

He shared effortlessly but it was a tool of manipulation. His tempting offer came with a price for the boys that accepted his 'generosity'. One mouthful and you owed him.

If you want to eat like a king, you have to work like a slave. That was his modus operandi.

The boys took the bait and he had them hook, line and sinker.

Truth be told, tricks like this and his success in the criminal world proved his entrepreneurial nous. He had strong leadership skills too. Some mornings I would wake up and there'd be eight kids, most no older than 14, waiting for him to emerge and give them their orders. Their lines of work were varied – petty theft, local drug dealing, burglary, county lines – but the rule from Ifaz was the same for them all: make at least £500 a day or you're in the shit.

And more often than not they did, for fear of Ifaz's disciplinarian action.

That was the most frustrating thing about working with Ifaz. He had all the tools to do something positive but he had tasted the street life and that was all he seemed to want, most of the time.

The police were regular visitors to the house after Ifaz came. They used to call him 'Baby Chino' in reference to mob movie stalwart Al Pacino. He was infamous around the city for his control of his crew, his baby face and pint-size frame, which belied his physical strength. One time the police came to the house to arrest him for robbery and it took six officers to restrain him.

Six.

Maybe I should have become wise to his ways but there were times when he appeared to have a change of heart and seemed to want to get on the straight and narrow. He'd spend hours in the library reading up on criminal justice and at one point he even attended college to study business studies. He was meticulous in his attendance and he soaked up the knowledge. But even there, he couldn't escape his past life.

This time, it wasn't other gang members but the police that made his life a misery. Every time he left the house to make his way to college they'd pounce on him like he was England's most wanted man. How could he even start to make a change when he was constantly being picked up? It infuriated me but with Ifaz, I had to accept there was no smoke without fire, no matter how much he pleaded that he was trying to leave the gang behind.

When college didn't work out, I got him some work on a building site. It only lasted two days. He wasn't one to take orders as he was far more used to giving them and he had a penchant for cannabis that didn't go down well with the site manager.

But at least he tried, I thought.

Surely his intentions were reason enough for *me* to keep trying to help him too? Other staff at the house gave Ifaz a wide berth. Some said he was a hopeless case; others said he was poisoning the rest of the house. Some were just scared of him. But I never gave up hope. I was certain I could help him even though he was so deeply embedded in the city's gang culture. I was convinced I could be the one to make a difference by daring to believe in him.

I stood beside him in the magistrates' courts as he told his tragic personal story, charming the judge into taking pity on him. I put my professional reputation on the line and vouched for him, time and again.

Then one day it all came crashing down.

About six months after he'd moved in, I was doing my weekly checks on the boys' rooms. When I opened the door to Ifaz's room, I tutted. It was a mess, with stuff strewn all over the floor. I started picking things up, to try to clear a path through, but as I looked closer I froze. This wasn't your usual teenage boy mess of sweaty trainers, dirty pants and the occasional bit of weed. It was mobile phones, credit cards and debit cards. Not just one or two but *dozens*.

Then, I spotted it. Rolled tightly and slid under the bottom corner of his bed frame. A wad of cash. I picked it up and gasped. There had to be at least a couple of grand there, rolled tightly and fastened with an elastic band. Behind it there was another, and another. In fact, they were all over the room.

As I continued rummaging under books and bedclothes, I found a small black notebook filled with numbers in Ifaz's angular handwriting. I frowned as I tried to make sense of the scribbles. It looked like code of some kind, or an account number . . .

Suddenly, I gasped. Like one of those magic eye puzzles sliding into focus, the numbers suddenly made sense. They were bank account numbers. *Foreign bank account numbers.*

If I wasn't mistaken, this was a book bursting with details of offshore accounts, where Ifaz was presumably stashing the cash

I was finding all over his bedroom. I counted more than ten thousand pounds before I stopped and put my head in my hands.

What have you done, Ifaz? I thought.

Suddenly things I'd seen and dismissed over the weeks and months made sense. The comings and goings at unsociable hours. Going missing for days on end. The way he'd been instantly popular with the other boys in the house and how they all snapped to attention when he was around.

He was grooming them.

Recruiting them, just like he'd been recruited.

Ifaz didn't spend his money on designer creps (expensive trainers) or gold. He was far shrewder than that. He provided for his family and invested in his business, showering the boys in the house with gifts. The food we'd seen, the flashy new trainers the other boys started wearing and the ready supply of skunk that seemed to be creeping into the house – it all now made sense.

Despite everything I'd hoped and worked for, he'd not moved away from his old gang life at all. Not for one minute. The changes of heart and attempts at an honest day's work had been part of a game. He'd been playing me, all while relocating his centre of operations to the house that I managed.

I knew what I had to do. I had to report him. But I wanted him to explain himself to me first. When Ifaz returned to the house that night, I was waiting for him in my office. I heard the floorboard creak outside in the hall and I called him in.

'Ifaz,' I said sternly. 'Can you come in here?'

'Yes, Chris, mate,' he replied, popping his head around the door.

'Can you explain all the money in your room?' I said. 'And the stolen credit cards and phones?'

Silence hung in the air as his eyes widened. I caught his gaze and I saw a rare nervous flicker. For once, he was on the back foot and he knew it.

He opened his mouth to speak but no sound escaped. I knew he wanted to tell me the truth but to do that would be betraying the code he lived by. If he broke that he'd be in far more trouble with the gang than he would be with me or the police.

'Please don't call the police, Chris,' he said. 'Please.'

'You know I have to,' I said, picking up the phone and dialling 999.

With that he nodded. You see, he knew the system. He knew what I had to do and he knew how that would end up for him. By the time I hung up the phone, Ifaz had gathered up the evidence and fled. You might catch him off guard but he was always still one step ahead. Of me, of his rival gangs and of the police. He knew when to walk the line and how to cover his tracks. He might get arrested but he'd never reveal the main operation because he wasn't your everyday thug. He was smarter. More calculating.

And fearless.

That was what made him the perfect recruit – and recruiter.

Weeks passed and I didn't see or hear anything of Ifaz. He'd been nothing but trouble for me but my stomach was still in knots as I thought about the implications my phone call might have had for him. Ifaz might have wielded some influence but the people above him didn't like it when their recruits got caught.

I imagined the potential domino effect. *The police cracking down, making arrests . . . Ifaz being taken out for betraying the gang . . . His parents getting the news he was . . .*

I stopped my train of thought and I shuddered.

He was far from an angel. Quite the opposite, in fact. But he didn't deserve that. And his parents certainly didn't.

Ifaz was the result of a system that bred anger out of injustice.

I managed to put him to the back of my mind until one day I got a call from Ifaz's social worker.

'He's been arrested for robbery,' he said. 'He's been sent to jail.'

'Thanks for letting me know,' I said.

It was a relief to know he was alive but that emotion was soon replaced by another.

Defeat.

I felt utterly defeated.

The sad truth about working with looked after children is that you can't save everyone. You can try your best to help them but sometimes it's just too late. I grabbed Ifaz at the edge of the cliff but he slipped through my fingers. What's more, while I was trying to pull him up, he was busy pulling other kids down, leading other boys in my care down the criminal path he had followed.

He was a prime example of one bad apple ruining the cart. What happens when the care system doesn't properly analyse the risk one resident could cause to others under the same roof. Once they're in, it becomes more difficult to weed them out. Once you see it happening, you report it. But for action to be taken it has to become a *real* problem. There's no nipping it in the bud. Social workers and the authorities didn't want the headache of finding another placement. And the service provider? A troubled boy like Ifaz was an excellent source of income.

Why on earth would I want to get rid of our cash cow? That was John's opinion when I flagged my concerns. He made it perfectly clear that I was to just do my job.

And my job was to sort it out or cover it up.

Reporting anything to anyone was like pissing into the wind. I was angry at Ifaz for deceiving me and for using my house as a point of recruitment, of course. But I never lost sight of why this had happened at all.

Because the system is fundamentally broken.

What if Ifaz and his family had arrived in the UK and were able to access better housing in a safer neighbourhood? What if his parents had been considered for the jobs that they did back in their home country and been paid a fairer wage? What if Ifaz hadn't seen his parents risk everything to bring him and his sister to a country where they were abused by a system that dehumanises and devalues refugees?

Would his story have ended differently?

More positively?

We'll never know how things might have turned out for Ifaz but I know for sure he will not be the last young person I see swallowed up into a life of crime because that's what the system sets you up for. As with county lines, prostitution or any form of street or gang crime, it's the poorest and most vulnerable young people who are prime targets for gang leaders.

Ifaz and Daniel were two sides of the same coin. One was a willing participant eyeing his way out of poverty, the other a desperate victim trapped by his vulnerabilities. But both were young people who witnessed nothing but deprivation and segregation all their lives and ended up trapped in the same vicious circle.

They were two stories that are replicated throughout the 2,500 active gangs in the UK. In the care sector, at some point, every young person swims towards the bait. But not everyone takes a bite. Either way, you lose. Those who refuse to conform are isolated, abused and bullied. Those who do, do so knowing there's no easy way to get out once you're in. You either pack your bags and leave town or die. So they adapt in order to survive and start seeking the next recruit, who will end up in the same cycle, which goes on and on and on . . .

That's the struggle we face daily in our job as care workers and one for which we don't have a solution because the issue is rooted so deeply in a wider problem. Gangs thrive on the visceral anger of being born into poverty, seeing destitution around you every day and watching the people you love suffer. The young people in the gangs that terrorise our streets are the ones that our government has beaten with the stick of austerity and abandoned. They've been left with no other option for survival than to be soldiers in a war that was never of their making.

CHAPTER SIX

Trafficking

Dardan

ANIMOSITY SEEPED FROM HIS pores as he spoke. It was an anger so deep that it could only have been born out of trauma. That much I knew. But I was only just beginning to understand the extent of what Dardan had been through.

He'd left Albania when he was just 14 years old, starting with the long journey overland to Calais before being bundled into a fridge in the back of a lorry by people smugglers, along with 12 other children from all corners of the globe. Like Dardan, they were all fleeing danger in their homelands and risking their lives to try to make it through the Channel Tunnel and emerge in England to a new, safer life.

'I was sat in the dark, crunched between two boxes. I couldn't move an inch. I didn't dare to in case we were caught,' he grimaced. 'I couldn't see anything except the whites of the other children's eyes. The whole journey, I wondered if I looked as scared as they did, because I was.'

'What were you most frightened of?' I asked.

Automatically, I assumed he'd fear death, suffocating on his way over. But for Dardan, there was a fate worse than death.

Being sent home.

'The longer we were in there, it felt harder to breathe. Like there was a weight on your chest that you couldn't push away. I just closed my eyes and prayed I'd never be returned to Albania.'

Dardan's father was a lawyer, and a good one at that. He'd played a part in bringing some of Albania's prolific gangsters to justice. But his success had come at a price. For each one he put away, he automatically put himself in debt to the gangs. He owed them in favours, money or – if he didn't comply – blood. The family has always been at risk because of Dardan's father's job but there was a thin line of security given his visible public role. He lived a good and careful life and sought only to keep his wife, two sons and two daughters safe.

But Dardan's older brother fell in with the gangs, like so many young men in the country did. He stole from them and ended up in a feud. To escape the repercussions, he upped and left the family home one night and fled the country. In doing so, he exposed the whole family to the risk of revenge – violence, murder or being trafficked and sold for sex.

His brother had left a debt that had to be paid.

His parents did the only thing they could do and sold all of their worldly possessions so they could send Dardan and his two sisters away from the country. He had no idea what had happened to his sisters but when Dardan emerged from that lorry into the darkness of the port at Dover he had a single focus – to get to London and start afresh. He scurried away from the travelling companions with whom he'd spent 48 hours cramped together, found a road and hitchhiked in the direction of the city.

'London, please,' he pleaded, using the few words of English that he knew.

Eventually though, he caught the attention of the police and was picked up and taken into custody until social services were contacted and the local authorities took over. His first foster placement, with a family in Luton, failed after six months.

'They were nice, good people,' Dardan told me. 'But they didn't trust me.'

'How do you mean?' I asked.

'They locked up all their things because they thought I would steal. They didn't let me eat dinner with them as a family because they didn't like me near their daughter. They thought I would sneak into her room at night to try to have sex with her,' he explained.

'Is that why you left?' I asked.

'I woke up one night and went to get a glass of water,' he said. 'When they heard me in the kitchen every light in the house went on and they all surrounded me, shouting and pointing. I couldn't communicate what I was doing . . . '

'So you got angry?' I asked.

Dardan nodded.

'I felt like I was in prison but I hadn't done anything wrong,' he said. 'A few days later, I went out and got drunk, which was against house rules. I came back so angry and said and did things I didn't mean. And that was that.'

I'd read about the incident in his notes. He'd threatened the family with a hammer.

It was inexcusable behaviour but also avoidable if he'd been put in the right kind of placement. There was no doubt the renumeration for taking Dardan on would have been a healthy amount. That was probably why they accepted him in the first place. But they weren't equipped to meet Dardan's needs. They were the kind of foster family where a runaway from a suburban British town would be well placed. Not a child who'd been smuggled thousands of miles from his family because his life was at risk.

They didn't have the tools to deal with the kind of trauma Dardan had experienced. They probably didn't even recognise it, but I did. The eyes never lied. They soaked up the truth like a sponge, capturing the perils of life and filtering the debris through the retina and straight to the heart. Trauma changed the whole body and took full control of your brain. That's why people made irrational decisions.

This lack of understanding was yet another failing of the system.

By the time Dardan was placed in my care, he was 16 and an orphan. Both of his parents had died two months after he'd left Albania; he never told me how and I wasn't even sure if he knew himself. He'd learned his brother was in Greece but didn't know what had happened to his sisters. I never said it to him but I had my suspicions and I suspect he did too.

Probably sold into the sex trade in Europe.

Unlike asylum seekers from other parts of the world, Dardan was relatively healthy. His life back home had been tough but never desperate. He told me that his mum always made sure there was food on the table. There wasn't a lot but there was always enough. It wasn't war or poverty he'd had to flee, it was Albania's political corruption and the organised gangs that were bleeding the country dry. He had no choice but to leave and build a new life for himself otherwise he would have had to spend the rest of his existence indebted to the criminal gangs chasing his brother.

He was the first and only Albanian boy in the house at the time. Despite arriving in the UK two years earlier, he was still awaiting his ARC card. So Dardan kept his head down. Finding himself in comparative comfort and safety, his anger began to dissipate. He would chat politely to the other boys in the house and spent hours practising his English, which had come a long way since he'd hitchhiked his way out of Dover. When I managed to get him on a basic English course, he was delighted. I worked with him daily on scripts that I'd written up myself and he never missed the opportunity to study them with me.

'Chris, today we do more English,' he'd say, as soon as I got into my office to start my shift.

'Yes, mate, later. Just give me chance to do my paperwork,' I smiled, heartened by his enthusiasm.

'OK, I wait here for you, until you done,' he said.

And he did. He would sit patiently in my office for hours and wait just in case I forgot. His college course was only two half days per week and without his ARC card he couldn't go far, so he had plenty of time to linger. When we weren't studying, he stood by me as I called the Red Cross, week after week, for news of his sisters.

So far there had been nothing. But he didn't give up. He was motivated by survival. If he wanted to progress and succeed in London; if he wanted to find out what had happened to his sisters he knew being able to speak English was a necessity. He knew that doing things by the book was the only way.

Maybe he got that work ethic from his father, I thought.

After a while I got a call from Dardan's social worker asking if we could take in another young Albanian boy. Even though Dardan's English was improving rapidly, he still struggled to communicate properly with the other boys in the house. He got on with them fine but it often felt like I was his only friend. I tried to work as many weekends as I could so that I could sit down and watch a movie or make some food with him and my staff supported him as much as they could during the week, but we all had our jobs to do as well. Having someone else who spoke his own language in the house would be a relief for Dardan, he'd have someone else to hang out with and it would take the pressure off me a little, so that the time I spent with Dardan could be dedicated, focused and beneficial. After thinking it over, I called Christian back and agreed to the new placement.

Argon's story was similar to Dardan's. He'd travelled over to the UK in the back of a lorry after fleeing Albania to escape the gangs. However, in contrast to Dardan, the account he gave of his journey was vague.

'The gangs want to kill me or sell me for sex so I left,' he said. 'I don't know how I got here; I was blindfolded until I arrived.'

There was something different about Argon. He *looked* every inch the terrified 16-year-old asylum seeker but he didn't act like one. Where Dardan was compliant but also jumpy, excitable and edgy at times, Argon was quiet and confident. When he spoke of his past it was without emotion, like a script tripping off his tongue. And I didn't see any of the visceral anger that I had in Dardan.

I frowned as I watched Argon head to his room with his small bag, Dardan tagging behind him like an obedient yet excited puppy.

What was his story, *really*?

The paperwork Christian had provided didn't reveal much more.

'There's not much else on him, mate,' he said apologetically.

I believed him. Christian was a good social worker. He did all the things that social workers supporting young people were *meant* to do – identify those in need, be there in crisis situations, help them find appropriate support and resources, work with young people to help them grow and develop the tools they need to move towards adulthood smoothly. The good ones didn't just dump their caseloads on new placements and run; they escorted them in, made introductions, checked the accommodation was suitable and stayed in touch until the point that young person was ready to leave. They advocated for their cases.

They gave a shit.

Christian gave a shit and that was why I never hesitated to take his placements if we had room. I knew he'd do things properly.

In the weeks that followed, I went through all the usual procedures that legally I had to follow, booking Argon in to see a doctor to be vaccinated, getting his eye test, taking him to the dentist and enrolling him in college.

I pressed gently in our key work sessions, trying to find out more about his situation, but his response was always the same: 'I left Albania because my life was in danger.'

He never spoke of family or friends. He never shared details of his childhood. It just felt like he was giving stock answers, like he was following a guide he'd bought: *How to get leave to remain in five easy steps.*

Something wasn't right but I couldn't pin down *what* exactly.

Argon and Dardan quickly formed a strong friendship but it wasn't an equal relationship between two peers. Argon was clearly the alpha male. It is the small nuances that give it away. Argon always walked through the door first and he entered with his chest puffed out. Dardan, on the other hand, followed behind him with his shoulders rounded and head down.

While Argon seemed to thrive, I noticed Dardan was quickly deteriorating. First it was his attitude. He stopped engaging in our keywork sessions, even the planned ones. I began to miss his quiet presence in my office as he eagerly waited to practise his English with me, all of his own volition.

Then the missing incidents started.

They would both vanish for days on end. Argon would look no different when they returned but Dardan would look dishevelled, thin, as if he hadn't eaten a mouthful since I'd last seen him.

When they came back it was always the same. Argon leading the way past my office without so much as an attempt at an apology or explanation. He'd just cockily saunter past as I called at them both to stop. Dardan never stopped but he always turned his head weakly in my direction and caught my gaze. I could see the desperation in his eyes. He wanted to reach out, to apologise, to ask for help. But he couldn't. Argon was always too close by, keeping Dardan in his sights. He never spoke, to me or to anyone in the house. His silence was like a fortress. An impenetrable wall behind which he was keeping Dardan captive.

When I noticed Dardan – who'd arrived with virtually nothing to his name and who couldn't work because of his immigration status – using a top-of-the-range iPhone, wearing new creps and having a plasma TV bolted to his wall, everything fell into place.

Argon was more than just an innocent unaccompanied minor.

He'd been sent from Albania by the very gangs that Dardan had fled to escape. Gangs that had got a foothold in UK territories, beaming back footage of their UK 'troops' living lives of luxury, wearing gold chains and brandishing fistfuls of cash, driving fast cars, drinking expensive liquor and being surrounded by beautiful women, thrusting and grinding in skimpy outfits.

They were idols to young men in Albania. They wanted to emulate them. They wanted a piece of that life. That was how the gangs recruited, with the promise of a life of wealth and luxury. Being untouchable. Being rock stars.

The reality that met these young recruits was far from the glamour they had been promised. The gangs in London recruiting them had interests in the county lines game. The Albanians needed constant fresh blood to peddle their wares up and down the country and what better source of recruits than home-grown talent?

Boys were smuggled over and given a script so well-rehearsed that it was impossible to see what was happening – at first, anyway. The weaker ones would be picked off, treated as mules, doing the dirty work on the ground. But the smarter ones, like Argon, saw a different route. Find more recruits for the gang, get *them* to do the work, while you enjoy the wealth.

I put my head in my hands and dug my nails into my scalp. *Poor Dardan.*

With his history, he probably had no option but to comply or risk revealing his father's job back home or his brother's indiscretions. If they found out who he was they'd most likely kill him. I could see what was happening but without any solid evidence with which to raise a concern, I felt powerless. Just like when I knew Ifaz was upsetting the balance of the house, it would take something serious for anyone to sit up and take notice.

As it happened, it wasn't long before the inevitable happened. I was off shift and I received a call from one of my night staff, Melissa.

'Argon and Dardan have been arrested,' she said. 'I know there's not much you can do now but I thought you'd want to know.'

The next day, I got into work two hours early, aware of the level of paperwork this kind of incident would generate. Most semi-independent providers do not pay too much attention to paperwork but I was meticulous. As the sun crept into the sky, more information emerged. The two boys had been stopped by the police on the motorway driving a brand spanking new BMW towards Devon. When they searched the vehicle, they found a few bags of Class A drugs, in a quantity sufficient to warrant armed police arresting them at gunpoint.

As I started to fill in the forms, the phone rang. It was Christian, calling from the police station.

'I'm bringing them back now,' he said. 'They've been bailed but need to attend court in a few weeks' time.'

Turns out the quantity of drugs seized wasn't sizable enough to keep them in custody. Being under 18 had helped as well.

'They're lucky,' I said, whistling through my lips. Lucky the police were more interested in breaking down the county line and getting to the big players, rather than the working ants.

When they arrived back at the house, Dardan looked devastated and even more scared than I imagined he had when he arrived in England. Argon was unaffected, of course. This was all par for the course for him.

'Are you alright, mate?' I said, deliberately directing my words to Dardan.

He nodded but he didn't look me in the eye.

I knew he felt ashamed. He was probably wondering what his dad would think of him. He probably thought that I was disappointed in him. But I wasn't. I was worried for him. I knew the Dardan who had existed before Argon came on the scene. I knew there was no way he would have taken such a big risk unless he was made to do so. I also knew what getting arrested meant for him.

If you lose the drugs, you pay for the drugs.

It wouldn't be Argon carrying that weight, I was sure of that.

Later that night, I found Dardan alone in the living room for the first time in months, away from the dark curve of Argon's shadow. I hadn't seen him since he'd gone to his room after returning from the police station. Still, I glanced around, just to be sure, before shutting the door and sitting beside Dardan on the couch.

'You have to walk away from this, Dardan,' I said. 'If you don't, the other options aren't good. You know that, right?'

He didn't speak but he looked at me, his eyes begging the question, 'What options?' His apparent naïvety was like a dagger to my heart.

'You'll end up dead or in jail,' I said, as gently as I could muster. 'Or they'll send you home.'

It was a reality I couldn't sugar-coat.

Dardan pulled his knees up to his chest and buried his face in them.

'If I go back to Albania, I'll go back in a box,' he said.

I nodded. I knew that going home would never be an option for him.

'We can help you, mate,' I said. 'But only if you let us.'

In the end, Argon never reappeared from his room. He left the house at some point during the night and never came back. It was clear why. The big boys had plans for him and they couldn't risk him getting locked up. Dardan was just a pawn, not worth saving.

Except, in a strange way, that's exactly what they did.

By taking Argon, they saved Dardan.

Fortunately, Dardan heeded my warnings. Freed from Argon's clutches, he managed to reconnect with the goals he'd had when he arrived – survival and success in the UK. He returned to his English course, which he eventually passed, and he dutifully made his appearance in court – without Argon, obviously – where he was given a 12-month conditional discharge. His solicitor explained how he'd been manipulated and acted under duress when the incident happened.

Like Yonah, when his ARC card finally arrived, so too did his freedom. Today, Dardan has permanent residency in the UK. He has a job, a flat of his own and plenty of friends. He's made a life here against all the odds, driven by the knowledge that the place he hails from is a place he'll never be able to call home again.

Telling his story, it feels strange to consider Dardan as one of the lucky ones. But his carriage into this country was not dissimilar to the articulated refrigerated lorry that became a coffin for 39 Vietnamese migrants, back in October 2019. Struggling to breathe, they'd made desperate calls to the outside world for help. Realising their fate, they'd then left heart-breaking goodbye messages for their families. When the vehicle was stopped in Purfleet in Essex, it was too late.

Twenty-nine men.

Eight women.

Two boys.

Thirty-nine lives snuffed out by a combination of hypoxia – a lack of oxygen to the lungs – and hypothermia. Killed by the traffickers profiting from bringing them illegally into Britain and the absence of any safe and legitimate alternative route to our shores. That could have easily been Dardan's fate.

He's lucky too to have escaped relatively unscathed from his brush with gang life. In the year that Dardan came to my house, I had three more boys come into my care who got involved with gangs and county lines, just as he had. Unfortunately, they were too far gone to rescue and their fate was already waiting for them in HMP Pentonville.

The UK National Crime Agency found that Albania was the biggest single source of people trafficking into the country, with

947 known cases referred to them in 2018 alone. This represents an increase of 50 per cent since 2015.[1] Many of these were sent by desperate families who had paid up to £10,000 to smuggling gangs to get their children to perceived safety in the UK. They believed – like Dardan's family did – that they were doing the best for them, all the while not realising that the people moving their children are part of the same criminal network as the gangs they were trying to keep them away from. In some cases they are one and the same.

These trafficking gangs brainwash their victims by promising them a better life if they do as they say and not as UK border forces, police and social services say. The young and vulnerable Albanians are told not to trust anyone in authority – or else. They comply out of fear.

The rest are young people sent by the gangs to extend their global reach. In many cases, they know exactly what they're coming for and exactly what they have to do when they arrive. They're exceptionally well-schooled. I learned the hard way just how wide and extensive their criminal networks were and the signs I needed to look for.

Corruption is a serious problem in Albania. It is one of the country's greatest stumbling blocks, impeding its bid for EU candidacy and hindering its investment climate. The procurement and construction sectors are particularly affected by patronage

---

[1] www.telegraph.co.uk/news/2019/11/10/albanian-parents-smuggle-children-uk-drug-trade/

networks and other forms of corruption. The judiciary is also hampered by corruption and political influence. The necessary anti-corruption legal framework is in place but enforcement is poor and conviction rates are extremely low – exactly the kind of environment where criminal entrepreneurship thrives.

There is already a sizable Albanian community in the UK, as many migrated to England after the Kosovo War in 1999 to escape the atrocities led by dictator Slobodan Milosevic, when they saw millions of their people slaughtered by Serbian and Yugoslavian soldiers. It goes without saying that not all in the Albanian community are part of this underworld – far from it. But the gangs have deep roots here and a code of conduct that is bound in blood.

No one informs, no one lies, and everyone is loyal to one another. Or you die.

This story is not unique to the Albanians. There is a similar trend in Somalian, Syrian and Turkish communities too, where vulnerable, disillusioned and angry young people have been recruited and sent to join a gang war on foreign shores. With so many of these young people arriving in the UK, there are simply not enough secure care homes to place them all. That's why local authorities end up placing most of them in unregulated accommodation, where they're free to come and go as they please and manipulate others to do their bidding.

As I've mentioned before, there is little you can do when you suspect a young person of being involved with gang life or county lines. You can report your suspicions to social services and/or the police and you log all the activity. But that's really about it. As a father, if I witnessed that kind of behaviour from my 16-year-old child, I would lock them in their bedroom and stop them from leaving the house until I could find a way to help them out of the danger they were placing themselves in. But if I did the same as a professional managing an unregulated provision, I'd be arrested. We have no power to make them stay at home. There's no Deprivation of Liberty order (DOLs) attached to the house. Any attempt to prevent residents leaving is considered holding them against their will.

Care homes have become easy targets because of the lack of safeguarding within the system. When young people come into semi-independent care or supported living between the ages of 16 and 18, they are classified as young adults. Yet if they lived at home with their parents and went to college, then they would be classified as children. The law protects one but forgets about the other.

It seems that the British government just doesn't seem to place any value on vulnerable children – because that *is* what they are – in the sector. They don't provide the powers or finance for us to provide proper care yet they wonder why so many young people go missing, are groomed into county lines or end up being killed in gang violence.

What I've also learned from experience is that if local authorities make a mistake – say, for example, putting a young person at risk by placing a gang-affiliated youth with others who might be vulnerable to manipulation, as was the case with Dardan and Argon – then it's quickly brushed under the carpet and you're expected to help with the tidy-up. But if a professional like myself was to go against the rules, even if it was in the interest of a resident's safety, they'd attack you all guns blazing and your career would be over.

What chance do we have of bringing about change? We're damned if we do and it's the kids who are damned if we don't.

CHAPTER SEVEN
The Staff

AS I WATCHED YOUNG people in my care cycle through the system, there were times when I found the houses I managed completely filled by boys who were involved in criminal activity and gang life. At times like this, the mood in the house was different but it didn't change my approach.

This is my house. When you step through these doors, it's a clean slate.

I got on with most of them well, probably because I didn't judge them for who they were or what they'd done. I also took my role in their lives seriously. As well as taking care of their wellbeing while they were under my roof, I wanted to do all that I could to steer them away from a life of crime. I believed everyone deserved a chance and that, given the right support, some of them would take it and turn their lives around.

Like I had done.

Unfortunately, not everyone felt the same. Leanne, another care worker, certainly didn't. She held the boys in nothing but contempt and made no effort to help them.

'Scum.'

That's what she and other staff of her mindset called the teenage boys in our care. Sometimes even within earshot of them. It infuriated me but she and her cronies were past me changing their minds so I focused my energy on doing my job and showing the boys they had an ally in me instead. That if they wanted help to change their course, I was there.

Though it was rarely easy. Respect between me and the boys had to be mutual and when it wasn't, I had to lay down the law. They had to abide by the house rules. If they didn't, it was my job to challenge them.

One night, I caught one of the boys smoking in his room. He was a gang-affiliated teenager who had been sent to us after he'd been arrested drug dealing and his mother had refused to have him back in her house. I'd spotted the faint plumes of smoke spiralling out of his window, marched straight upstairs and knocked on his door.

'Josh, you know you're not supposed to smoke in the house, it's a fire hazard,' I shouted. 'Can you put it out and take it outside, please?'

'Fuck off,' came the reply.

Instinctively I rolled my eyes. It wasn't unusual, aggression was often their first line of defence. On the streets it was all they knew. But I wasn't going to stand for that. I knocked again.

'I'm not going away. You know the rules,' I said. 'Put it out or go outside.'

'FUCK OFF!' came the response again.

It irked me slightly but I knew that rising to him wouldn't work. Undeterred, I carried on.

This was my house and these were my rules.

'Josh. Outside. Now,' I said firmly.

This time, he didn't shout back. I heard the rustling of a sports jacket being angrily pulled on and trainers being stomped into. Then the door clicked and I stepped back.

Josh emerged, scowling, with a half-smoked, extinguished cigarette hanging from his lip.

'Alright, I'm going,' he huffed.

'Thank you,' I said, before I turned on my heel and headed back to the office. Leanne was on duty and it was my responsibility to report any verbal altercation with a young person, so it could be recorded.

'I just had to have a word with Josh about smoking in his room,' I said casually.

It wasn't a big deal. It was just important that the whole team knew what had happened on each shift. I was prepared for her response. Leanne's dislike of the boys usually meant she'd give a snide comment or two. Sometimes she'd push to see if anything more had happened – something she could twist into reporting to their social workers, anything to make their lives that little bit more miserable. But usually I was able to talk her down.

'What happened?' she asked.

'He was smoking, I asked him to stop. He told me to fuck off a couple of times, then I asked again and he went outside as requested,' I said. 'It's all sorted.'

'That's it?' she said, her face going beetroot with anger. 'You let him walk out after speaking to you like that?'

'I didn't see the benefit of creating conflict,' I replied. 'He did what was asked of him.'

Leanne got up and stomped across the office, fists clenched by her sides. She slammed the door shut and turned to face me. She was like a pot reaching the boil as she stared at me momentarily. Then her rage bubbled over.

'Don't give him any of your time, do you hear me?' she screamed. 'He's a street rat and the best place for him is jail.'

My jaw dropped open.

'What the fuck are you talking about?' I said. 'It was a minor disagreement and in the end he did the right thing.'

'I don't give a shit,' she replied, grabbing the phone from the desk.

'What are you doing?' I asked.

'I'm calling the police,' she said.

My face contorted with confusion. The police weren't going to come round to deal with a verbal altercation – if you could even call it that – which had been resolved. It would be a waste of everyone's time . . .

'Hello,' Leanne said, when the operator answered. 'I'd like to report an incident.'

Ridiculous, but she's giving it a go, I thought.

There was a pause as she waited for an officer to pick up. I crossed my arms as she started to speak, shaking my head as I watched.

'Hello, officer. A young person in our care has just attacked one of my members of staff because he asked him to stop smoking in his bedroom,' she said.

My heart started racing and instinctively I yelled out.

'The boy didn't attack me,' I shouted, stepping forward in the hope the officer would be able to hear me. Leanne raised her hand and put it an inch away from my face, scowling between the gaps in her fingers.

'*Shut up,*' she mouthed.

'Fuck that!' I responded.

But it was too late, the report had been made and the police were on their way.

'They said they'd be here in no time. They've put an urgent call out,' she said calmly, avoiding any eye contact.

'Leanne, what the fuck are you doing?' I said, trying to keep my voice at an acceptable level. 'Are you crazy? He did not attack me. You know he didn't. I don't want to get the poor boy locked up.'

'Poor boy? POOR BOY?' she shouted, making no attempt to keep a level tone. 'He's a criminal and scum.'

'But he didn't do anything wrong here!' I shouted back.

Leanne turned and glared at me. If looks could kill, I'd have been stone dead. She didn't like me challenging her authority but I didn't care. I wasn't going to allow someone to be locked up for telling me to fuck off.

'Don't talk to me like that or I'll have you fired,' she hissed.

'Go for it,' I said. 'Tomorrow morning I will be contacting the boy's social worker and filing a complaint against you.'

I stood my ground, shoulders back and head high, confident that it was her in the wrong, not me. Suddenly, her face softened and a pink flush began to creep up her neck and across her cheeks.

'Listen, Chris,' she said softly, 'I'm just trying to make your shift easier.'

Here we go, I thought. *Backtracking to save her own skin.*

'You can see I'm trying to help,' she nudged.

As if I even needed her help. I rarely had a problem on my shifts and if I did, I wasn't calling the police every five minutes. She continued to stare at me, waiting to back down but I didn't dignify her feeble attempt to placate me with a response.

I preferred to let her stew.

As soon as the police arrived, I did my best to explain that there had been a mistake. There had simply been an exchange of words – no physical violence, not even close.

'There's been a misunderstanding,' I pleaded as they barged past me and up the stairs to Josh's room. 'I've already dealt with the incident but my colleague wasn't aware.'

But they didn't want to listen.

This boy, Josh, was known to them. Any squeak of him stepping out of line and they were more than happy to come in mob-handed. I followed behind them and watched helplessly as they forced their way into his bedroom and dragged him to the floor.

'Get off! What the. . . ?' he screamed.

He didn't know what had hit him.

One minute, he was sat on his bed, listening to music; the next, six police officers were piling on top of him. He was under attack and he had no idea what for.

So what did he do? He lashed out, of course. As he tussled with the officers, he swore and threw punches, until eventually he landed one square in an officer's face. His reaction wasn't surprising. I didn't blame him because any normal human being would have done the same thing.

But kids in care with a criminal record aren't treated like 'normal'. Often they aren't even treated like human beings.

I watched the officer's colleagues hold Josh back as a trickle of blood escaped from the policeman's left nostril and ran onto his white shirt, and I shook my head. He was in for it now.

Josh was still shouting and screaming as they read him his rights, dragged him downstairs like a rag doll and threw him in the back of the waiting police van. I sighed as I watched it screech away. It didn't matter what I said or did now, the fact that the incident they turned up to deal with was completely fake was irrelevant. A police officer was injured and the damage was done.

She was the last person I wanted to see, but as I turned into the office, there she was, sitting at her desk, grinning smugly.

Leanne.

This had all been her doing. And she didn't give two hoots.

'I told you he was dangerous,' she smirked.

There was so much I wanted to say but I bit my tongue and blanked her. The only time I spoke to her for the rest of my shift was to refuse to sign the incident report she had written. I didn't even need to read it to know it would be full of lies.

'It's false, so it's illegal,' I said curtly. 'I won't be signing it.'

She huffed and tossed the papers onto my desk.

The next day was my day off but I couldn't put the incident to the back of my mind. A young man had been detained unfairly. I couldn't let that happen. Despite his record and gang affiliation, Josh was a good kid and had been making progress in the house. He wasn't always compliant, but show me a teenager that is. He had been trying and he'd been giving me no trouble at all. I emailed his social worker to explain how the incident had actually unfolded in the hope that we could provide something in his defence.

He did nothing wrong and the police acted inappropriately. Please get in touch so that we can work together to rectify this, I typed.

He never got back to me.

In the end, Josh was charged with resisting arrest and assaulting a police officer, things that would never have happened if Leanne had trusted my judgement and had his best interests at heart. But she didn't. She was spiteful, lacked empathy and, in my opinion, she was unfit to be in a caring role.

As well as having it in for the kids, now she had it in for me too. It wasn't the first time that I'd seen this side of the industry but it was the first time in this particular house. A few days after the incident, I received a call from John.

'There has been a complaint about you, Chris,' he said.

'Oh really, from who?' I asked, even though I already knew.

'Leanne,' he said. 'She said that you called her a crazy bitch.'

I shook my head in disbelief. *I'd asked if she was crazy, because she'd just told the police a barefaced lie.*

She was a piece of work. Twisting words to suit her agenda. Lies slipped off her tongue like butter off a hot knife.

'She said she doesn't want to work with you again because you make her feel inadequate and she said you're condescending.'

At that point, I had to stifle a laugh. If she felt inadequate, it was because she *was*. If I was condescending then it was because I didn't think she should be working with vulnerable young people.

I'd told her as much – and with good justification too. So I repeated my concerns to John.

'I've told you before, she's not fit for the role,' I said.

John sighed. 'You need to find a way to work together,' he said. 'We can't let her go.'

'Why not?' I pushed.

'She's been with us for a long time,' he said. 'She knows how our houses operate. You know . . .'

As he tailed off suddenly I understood.

She knows where all the bodies are buried, I thought.

I'd only worked in a handful of John's houses. Yes, they were clean; yes, they were safe in comparison to others I'd seen, but they were all about profit and I know that not everyone was like me. Not everyone called out inappropriate placements, poor facilities – or lies about young people that resulted in unnecessary arrests. There were clearly things that she knew that could destroy John and his businesses, so he had to do his best to keep her onside.

In the public sector, an incident like the one with Josh would have triggered weeks and weeks of investigations, scrupulous interviews, meetings with heads of departments and managers. If heads needed to roll then they did.

But not in the private sector. They tried to keep it all in house, brush it under the carpet and find ways to keep anyone who might be able to reveal their secrets quiet. A healthy salary usually seemed to do it, along with free rein to destroy the lives of young people in their care.

The incident with Leanne was the first time that I'd ever had to deal with a completely fabricated incident, created out of spite. But it wasn't the first time the police had to come and deal with an altercation between a resident and staff member on my watch.

Working in semi-independent provisions where there is no regulation and usually a prevailing profit-over-people approach is difficult. Especially when you give a damn and want to do things properly. There are always tough judgement calls to make.

As the house manager, I was called into work one day after a care worker had been verbally assaulted by a young person. They had apparently retaliated by punching the resident in the face. When I arrived, I spoke to the care worker. He broke down and confessed that he had lashed out. He told me that this particular young person had been making their life a misery and – at breaking point – he said he'd just snapped.

Of course, the young person's version was different.

He claimed he'd gone to the office and asked if he could use the phone and he had attacked him, unprovoked.

After that, the story spiralled out of control. The care worker went from confessing their misdemeanour to pleading self-defence. His story changed; he was now saying the young person had followed him into the office and tried to take the phone off him. He claimed that the young person had spat in his face and then attacked him.

'I acted in self-defence,' he asserted. 'The young person attacked me first.'

The story was completely different from the confessional he'd given me when I first arrived. I'd known there was some history and tension between the two. I'd raised it with my bosses, even asking that the care worker be moved to another house to reduce the chances of an incident, a request they refused. I knew that either version of events could be true, or somewhere in between the two. But with the information I had and no cameras in the office to confirm either one's story, I couldn't make head nor tail of what happened.

I had to call the police. I was all for giving the benefit of the doubt but any form of assault – against resident or staff member – had to be investigated and dealt with properly.

I told the care worker to start writing out his incident report while I took a statement from the young person. He said that he retaliated only because he was provoked. When I asked him if he spat at the staff member he said yes, because he was angry. When the police finally arrived, I told them what I knew and they spoke separately to both the young person and the staff member.

Much as with Josh, when the police arrived, the boy was riled. I struggled to keep him calm and explained that the police were there to listen to both parties fairly but I think I knew deep down that he would always be at a disadvantage.

My instincts were right.

In the end, the young person was arrested for assaulting the care worker. The police felt there was sufficient evidence that he had forced his way into the office and started the attack. I had to accept their judgement but I struggled to forget the indications of guilt in what the staff member originally told me.

When the incident report, which was to be sent to the resident's social worker, came back from my director I glanced over it. It bore no resemblance to the original report. It was sanitised and biased completely in favour of the staff member. Any slight shades of guilt or responsibility had been erased. I could almost hear John's voice in my ear.

Well, we wouldn't want the local authorities who pay our wages thinking we couldn't do our jobs now, would we?

I didn't have the authority to challenge my director. The times that I did speak up, suggesting more appropriate procedures that promised better protection and outcomes for staff and residents alike, I'd been ignored. It was evident that they did not like reporting things to the Local Authority Designated Officer (LADO) or other external agencies whose job it was to investigate these kinds of things.

In any other regulated professional setting, regardless of the outcome of the police visit, the staff member would have been suspended pending investigation. But this generally didn't seem to happen in private houses. Private companies did not want to tarnish their reputation. An ongoing investigation into a staff member could put off a new authority looking to place its most vulnerable – read 'profitable' – children, which could easily put a dent in a company's income. I guess that explained why they preferred to keep everything behind closed doors.

What's more, we couldn't afford to be losing care workers, no matter what.

We were always teetering on being understaffed. I was often on shift alone, something that would never happen in a regulated provision and something I knew was risky but still did.

Because we had no choice.

In the private sector, where profit is king, there's little interest in following robust procedures or paying for good staff. Instead, private homes churn through unsuspecting and low-paid graduates who leave within weeks, if not days, because – for all their academic qualifications – they are woefully underprepared for the realities of the job.

Then there's the unqualified staff who despite being employed as care workers, key workers and even managers – because formal training isn't essential in private provisions – are paid such a meagre wage there is no incentive for them to even try to provide proper support. For the appalling pay they receive, I don't believe any amount of passion could motivate them to deliver the work that's needed. They're either glorified babysitters looking for an easy ride, watching Netflix and raiding the house fridge or hiding in the office for the duration of their shift because they are scared and not trained to deal with what is going on around them.

When provisions *do* chance upon good staff, with appropriate experience and a real commitment to providing proper, professional support to young people, they refuse to pay for quality. I once introduced an experienced and passionate care professional to John for the role of manager in one of his houses. Despite being quite young, she was exceptionally well trained, had bags of experience and was committed to the sector. I was really hopeful that he would take on my recommendation and give her the job because I thought she'd be a breath of fresh air. I was so excited that I called her as soon as I knew the interview was done.

'How did it go?' I asked.

'Chris, I'm sorry but I laughed in their faces,' she said. 'It was a joke.'

'What happened?' I asked, deflated.

'They offered me £7 an hour,' she said. 'To manage that house.'

I felt my cheeks prickle red.

Minimum wage, with her experience and skills?

What were they thinking? Never in a million years did I think he'd try and palm off a seasoned care worker with minimum wage. I thought he was smarter than that. I was mortified. She moved in respected, professional circles. I was worried that if word got out, the company's reputation would be in tatters. And so would mine – I'd encouraged her to apply after all.

What they could have done that day is the same thing that other provisions up and down the country could do every day – make an investment. Instead, what happens is they look at the steady flow of more unreliable – but much, much cheaper – staff and make a decision: profit first. Not people.

And it shows.

As the saying goes – pay peanuts, get monkeys.

Sometimes it was hard to distinguish who was unsuitable for the job, who did work that reflected their rate of pay and who was just taking the piss. There were constant rumours floating around about workers being paid £6 per hour – less than minimum wage – being employed without a DBS check to review their background and see if they had a criminal record, or sometimes even both.

During my time in the semi-independent sector, I found that too many processes and procedures, which were in place for the safety of both young people and staff, were being ignored. I didn't want to work in places that didn't do things correctly, putting all of us at risk. I didn't want to work with people who would manipulate, lie and stab you in the back, all in pursuit of making their own lives easier or better. To me, that wasn't what the job was about.

It was this absence of team unity, the lack of support and genuine care for the young people, and the risks we faced on a daily basis that wore me down. I knew that it was doing the same to other committed workers too.

There were – and still are – lots of good people who work in the private sector, are passionate and genuinely want to make a difference. These people should be rewarded with a good salary, training and a safe, supportive working environment. But these things cost money and many directors don't want to spend a penny on nurturing quality staff members. So what you end up with is houses staffed by people who don't care or make mistakes that could potentially put young people at risk. Either way, the burden of responsibility falls on the most committed, experienced and usually most exhausted and disillusioned staff.

Combine low pay and high pressure with a lack of training, support and regulation, add a dose of greed and obsession with profit from the 'powers that be' and you're left with a very unsafe and toxic environment. The only ones who escape unscathed are the company owners and directors in their ivory towers with their six-figure salaries. As a manager, I tried to exercise the little bit of authority and influence that I had. To stand up and call out where things were going wrong. But to little avail. Everything I saw as a win opened up a chasm between myself and my superiors.

When you speak up against the system, you put a target on your own back. Those who may have seen me as a co-conspirator in their quest for wealth and success soon marked me out as the enemy, after I refused to turn a blind eye to the corruption and greed in businesses that had the audacity to call themselves providers of 'quality care'.

I saw and witnessed things I could not keep quiet about. The majority of the young people I worked with I genuinely cared about. Even the ones who were well past my help, I maintained my professional obligation to. My role was to make sure they were safe and well, both mentally and physically, but the environment that the private ownership structure created made it nigh on impossible.

The staffing issues I witnessed are replicated today in privately run semi-independent provisions across the UK. Low-paid and untrained staff are being led by directors who do not care about anything apart from the business's bank balance. Managers either keep their office doors closed and offer nothing in support to the young people on their care or – like Leanne – flex their authority and make life difficult for them.

Staff issues are the creaking foundations of the system's crumbling structure.

Most young people in care, as they are moved from home to home, never know what they're going to get from their next house manager or care worker.

An apathete or authoritarian.

Left to their own devices or ruled with an iron fist.

Supported or sacrificed.

With no consistency in this so-called 'system' and no investment in its staffing, young people are bound to rebel against it because it makes no sense at all. While it's fair to say that care workers, particularly the lower paid, have a lot to contend with, it's also fair to say that the people at the top have the power and the means to improve things for both staff and residents.

There is another way. Like investing in appropriately trained staff and following proper processes and procedures when incidents arise. Using the flexibility of the unregulated system to allow young people some freedoms within strictly defined boundaries. Allowing knowledgeable staff – paid well for their expertise – to make decisions that will foster a healthier living *and* working environment.

But they don't want to because this approach narrows the profit margins.

While the incidents that will continue to arise out of the strain caused by this endemic underfunding will be uncomfortable and unpleasant for those working in the sector, it will still be the young people in the care of the system who will find themselves worst off.

CHAPTER EIGHT

Nothing Changes

THE LONGER I WORKED in private houses, the more issues I saw unfolding before my eyes. I was earning a good living and I was trying my best to do what I could to tackle the problems as I found them, but the more responsibility I gained, the more complicit I became. I began to see my part in it all and I didn't like it.

One night, John told me he wanted to discuss the business with me. As we sat having a *tête-à-tête* about politics and business, I suddenly remembered something. We'd just taken in a new resident and I needed to speak to John about his living arrangements.

'We need to move Tesfay into another room,' I said.

'Why, what's wrong with the one he has?' John asked.

'He complained to his social worker about the slanted roof. He can't stand up straight in there,' I said.

I was bending the truth a little. Tesfay was a 16-year-old boy from Sudan. He'd come to England seeking asylum and had spent the last two years of his life sleeping on a cold, hard floor in a refugee camp in Calais. The only room free in the house was the attic room that had space for little more than a single bed and chest of drawers. It wasn't a bedroom, it was a cupboard, and after everything he'd been through, I felt he was entitled to have some comfort in his new home.

Tesfay hadn't complained as such; it had been mentioned in passing. But I could see how uncomfortable he was, stooped awkwardly at the narrow end of the room, clutching his bag of worldly possessions. I am five foot eight and I had to contort like a pretzel in there. He was two inches taller than me so I could only imagine how frustrating it would be for him.

He was just glad to have safety and shelter. But that wasn't good enough for me. It wouldn't do for one of our UK care leavers, who would have recoiled in horror at the sight of it, so why should it be OK for an asylum seeker? They were all kids, with the same basic needs: food, safety, support and comfort.

When I'd suggested in the past that the room wasn't really a suitable place for a young person to live, I'd been brushed off. For John, an extra room meant another resident and another monthly payment from some local council. It was another way to maximise the profit on our space.

John laughed. 'What should I do, Chris?' he said. 'Should I knock the roof down and rebuild it myself?'

It was exactly the response I'd expected.

'Well, no. But I just thought, with Ifaz gone, we could move him into his room?'

'Is the room we have given him worse than what Tesfay has had to endure in his past?' John sneered. 'Is it not up to his standards?'

That's not the point, I thought.

But I didn't want John to think I was being a nuisance. I didn't want him to question my business acumen or think I was too swayed by my emotions. As if reading my mind, John started speaking again.

'You have to understand, Chris, that sometimes in business only money can make things happen,' he said. 'If this boy wants a bigger room then the local authority need to pay me more money.'

As those last four words tripped from his lips he let out a hearty laugh. And instead of challenging him, instead of challenging the system that I knew was broken, I laughed too. You see, I knew that was how it worked. In this industry, the only language these people understood was money. My heart spoke a different tongue, one of compassion and care. But that wouldn't get me anywhere with John. If I wanted to make my way in this business, I was going to have to talk their talk and do as they did.

At least when I was among them.

Day-to-day at the house was a different matter. John didn't allow a penny to be spent on anything that wasn't essential or an investment that would yield some form of profit. He even refused budget for a chocolate bar and bottle of water to be placed in the room of any new resident arriving as a way to say 'welcome'. I paid for stuff like that out of my own pocket, as well as things like takeaways, additional food shopping and treats. They were all little things that made a colossal difference to the boys. Seeing their eyes light up at the sight of a KFC bucket or jumbo bag of Haribo could make my day.

I was conflicted. I wanted to be the best I could. A businessman and a changemaker. But after that conversation with John, I couldn't sleep for thinking about how I'd laughed at his insensitive joke.

They'll need to pay me more money.

I needed to do something to bring myself some equilibrium, to do the right thing for Tesfay *and* keep John's profit margins healthy. So I called Tesfay's social worker.

'We can put him in a bigger, much nicer room if we can get a little extra budget,' I explained. 'It will be much more comfortable for him.'

'If he doesn't like his room then what can I do?' she said bluntly. 'There's no money for luxury here.'

I tried to explain that it wasn't about luxury. It wasn't like I was a hotelier trying to upgrade someone for a few extra quid. It was just an appropriately sized bedroom. But she didn't give a toss. He was in a house and looked after. That part of her job was complete. Ticked off.

I churned over what to do for days. Every time I saw Tesfay, stepping into his room already hunched over or rubbing his aching back, I was wracked with guilt. It just wasn't right. It didn't take long before my moral compunctions got the better of me.

John had made it clear this was *my* house. He left me to my own devices in every other sense so why was I not calling the shots now? I knew everything was a test. I'd be judged on my suitability to run the business with every choice I made.

Well, fuck it – I am the boss here and it is my call.

It didn't take long to move him. He only had a few items of clothing and bedding to gather. I guided him down the corridor and opened the door to the only other vacant room in the house.

'This is your room now,' I said. Tesfay's eyes almost popped out of his head, like in a cartoon.

'Oh, Mr Chris, thank you so much,' he said, mouth open in disbelief.

My heart almost cracked at his reaction. It was a small, square room with a single bed, a wardrobe and chest of drawers. And enough space to stand up straight.

The next day I called John and told him. He didn't say much but I could tell he was disappointed.

'What next, a car?' he said indignantly.

'It was the right thing to do, John,' I said firmly.

'You're too soft,' he muttered.

I knew I could have fought back but it was a battle I'd never win. Not there and not then anyway.

As the months passed, I found it harder and harder to do the things that were required of me as a businessman. Once I realised I was complicit, I scrutinised every action and refused to put profit before people. How could I?

As well as working my hours for John, I was travelling the country delivering keynote speeches, visiting schools, conferences and hosting charity events that were supporting organisations fighting for the rights of young people in care. I was stood on a pedestal claiming to be the voice of lived experience, speaking for all those kids in the system now who couldn't speak for themselves, all while I was part of the machine that was gagging them.

In the end, it was an email that reminded me where I belonged. What side I really wanted to be on.

It was 2am when my phone buzzed. It was a direct message on Twitter. Despite the fact it was the middle of the night, I clicked it open and was reading it before my brain caught up with what I was doing.

Dear Chris.

My name is Rebecca and I've just finished reading Damaged. I couldn't put it down. It took me two days to read it all. I don't usually read books but I had to read yours. I was in a children's home when I was 13 because my mum was a druggie. I was there for a year then I went to live with my dad. He had problems too but my social worker didn't give a shit and he wanted someone to be his servant. My dad abused me and I've never been able to talk about it until I read your book. I can relate to the girls you talk about and I've been thinking about ways to kill myself. But now I've read Damaged I'm going to ask for help and get my dad arrested. Anyway, you probably won't reply but I thought I'd give it a go.

Rebecca

There were eight words in that message that sent me from 0 to 100 in a matter of seconds: *I've been thinking about ways to kill myself.*

Suddenly, I was wide awake and my heart was hammering in my chest at such a rate that I could barely catch my breath. I didn't even pause to think as I fired off a reply with my phone number.

Call me please. I need to make sure you're OK, I typed.

I hit send and waited but nothing happened.

Oh God, what if I was too late? I panicked.

I didn't know what else to do so I started shaking Androulla awake.

'Androulla, look at this,' I said.

'What is it?' she said, rolling over.

I handed her my phone with the email still open.

'She says she's thinking about killing herself. What should I do?' I asked. 'Should I call the police?'

I could hear the panic and urgency in my voice. It was as if someone's life depended on me. I guess because I kind of felt like it did. I held my breath as Androulla read the message.

Say something, I willed as she read it again. And another time.

'First of all, take some deep breaths. Secondly, she hasn't said she's going to kill herself. She said she was thinking about it but now she's going to get help instead.'

Typical Androulla, with her rational thinking cap on. She is the exact opposite to me – bag of anxiety that could take a pebble, make it into a mountain, then add a hurricane and a few tornadoes for good measure.

Her calm response soothed me and when Rebecca didn't reply to my message asking her to call me, I wrote her a more detailed message in reply instead.

Thanks for your message, Rebecca. It really touched me. I want you to know that you are never on your own. I've had many moments where I want to call it a day but somehow I manage to hold on. We are the minority because we survived. That is what makes us stronger than anyone else. Please, if you need to talk then call me, even if it's 2am, I don't care. Although we are not related we are a family and I'm always here to help, when and where I can. I want you to contact me tomorrow and I will help you find someone to talk to.

Chris x

But the next day she didn't call me either and she even deleted her Twitter account. I was a mess and just couldn't put it out of my mind. Ever the sensible one, Androulla had a solution again.

'Speak to a professional about this,' she advised. 'Tell them what happened and get their advice.'

'I'll call Patrick,' I said.

Patrick is a child psychologist, a friend and – in my eyes – a living legend. I'd known him since I started working in care homes and we'd became really good friends as well as professional colleagues when the children in my care needed his services. He is the kind of person who has the ability to take your problems, help you break them down into microscopic particles, then put them into the palms of his hands and blow them away into infinity and beyond.

I needed some of that just then.

As accommodating as ever, when I asked if I could go round to see him, he welcomed me with open arms. Twenty minutes and a short drive up the A10 later, I was in his picturesque little cottage filled with thousands of books, lying all over his tables, chairs and floors and spilling from his shelves.

I knocked gently on his door and he invited me in. I sat down in a chair facing his and as he reclined into his seat, I blurted out everything that was in my head.

'Patrick, I need your advice and maybe your help. It's urgent,' I said, showing him the screenshot of the message on my phone, along with my replies.

Patrick took his time to analyse the text, then he handed me my phone back and gazed at one of his bookshelves for a moment. After what felt like an eternity, he spoke.

'I think you did the right thing. Your message was clear and precise and I would have done the same,' he said.

'Are you sure?' I asked.

'Yes,' he said. 'This is what comes with writing a book about your life. You expose your vulnerability to the masses and people resonate with that. You have to be honest and willing to listen when people respond.'

'That was always the plan,' I said. 'I wanted my story to give others the confidence to get help.'

'Well, it seems to be working,' he smiled.

As I drove home, I thought about what he'd said and I realised just how far from my original mission I'd strayed and how much I wanted to get back on track. Trying to change anything from my place in the care sector ivory tower of management was like banging my head against a brick wall. The people around me weren't interested and the people above definitely didn't want to hear it.

My relationship with John and Cesar was becoming strained as I spent more and more time focusing on the 'caring' aspect of my role. I built up a list of contacts, charities and support groups so I could direct people like Rebecca to help more effectively. I had professionals and good Samaritans contacting me on Twitter, asking if they could help the young people I worked with, by sending money or necessities. When Christmas came round, I put together over a hundred gift boxes and distributed them to children's care homes all around the country.

It was the most rewarding thing I'd done in a long time.

Maybe ever.

As my anger towards the sector grew, so too did my reputation for speaking the truth on social media, which grabbed the attention of two BBC journalists called Katie Razzall and Sally Chesworth. They were conducting an investigation into the way children in care were treated in the UK and they contacted me to ask if I would be willing to speak to them about my experience in both unregulated and unregistered provisions. The investigation was for a BBC *Newsnight* series called *Britain's Hidden Children's Homes* and it would touch on every single broken part of the system – illegal provisions where children were neglected and abused, county lines and grooming, profiteering private businesses and the unscrupulous councils trying to save a few pennies at the expense of young people's wellbeing and safety.

I agreed immediately. If my experiences had helped others in the past then they could do again. When I met with Katie and Sally in London for my interview, I explained exactly why I was doing it.

'This is personal to me,' I said. 'I have experienced it first-hand and on both sides. I'm doing it for all the young people who are *still* living in fear because of our dysfunctional care system.'

After an initial chat, they sat me in a chair in the middle of a vast recording studio, where I waited to be interviewed. I thought about what I was going to say and how I was going to get my point across succinctly. I wanted people to understand what was happening in the care sector and how young people were being abandoned by those in authority who were supposed to keep them safe. If I'd really let rip, I probably would have just screamed my frustration at the camera but I had to keep my composure.

But as soon as the interview got underway, Taylor popped into my head. His face at the sight of a made bed and the stories of how he'd been treated before. A switch flipped and my emotions got the better of me as I recounted his story, fighting back tears as I did.[1]

We all have those life-changing moments that make us question our purpose. As the saying goes, by changing nothing, nothing changes. I knew as I sat in that seat, I couldn't hide behind a salary anymore. Being well paid wasn't worth being complicit in a system that I knew was fundamentally flawed.

If I'm being honest, I thought I'd messed up my opportunity. I'd become so upset telling Taylor's story that I wasn't even sure if they'd use my interview. But they did and the response was overwhelming. My clip received over two million views online. The series was viewed by millions more and – most importantly – it was seen by the right politicians, who could no longer ignore the stories as hearsay.

After the series aired, the children's commissioner for England, Anne Longfield, spoke to BBC *Newsnight* and said that the government should ban placing under-18s in care in unregulated homes in light of concerns over sexual and criminal exploitation.

Like what happened to Daniel, Dardan and Ifaz.

A government consultation was launched on proposals to introduce new minimum standards to the care sector, where one in eight children spent time in an unregulated home in 2018–19. The Education Secretary, Gavin Williamson, also commented on the investigation, saying that, 'The BBC highlighted something that just needed to be changed.'

---

[1] www.bbc.co.uk/news/av/uk-49963269

And he was right, it did.

But I'd realised, after two years of trying, that I was never going to manage that from the inside. I handed my notice in to John, packed up my things and decided to find a more effective way to make an impact. I had all the experience I needed in the care sector; I'd seen everything I needed to see from every possible angle and after two years working for John in the semi-independent care sector, it was now time to move on.

CHAPTER NINE

History Repeats

Desire

SOMETIMES IT TAKES A step backward to free yourself enough to move forward in the direction you want to be moving. In the turmoil of breaking away from my work in private houses in the semi-independent care sector, I found myself drawn magnetically back to where my journey in the system began.

Back home to Halifax.

Like Rebecca, Desire slipped into my life through private messages on social media. She too had read *Damaged* and reached out to share her story with me. But unlike Rebecca, who vanished after I replied, Desire wanted to continue the conversation.

After months of messaging, we arranged to meet. It always happened like this. Once people shared their story, prompted by my own, I became a part of it and felt a responsibility to them.

Solidarity in shared trauma.

The café she suggested was inconspicuous and tucked away in a corner within a corner of Halifax town centre. A bell rang when you pushed the door open, a throwback to cafés of old, but everything else had been modernised to keep up with

Halifax's shiny new cosmopolitan image. Its walls were tiled like a monochrome Rubik's cube but the rest of the décor was loud, with iridescent pink chairs and rainbow tablecloths laughing at the minimalist palette it was laid against.

'It's an easy place to hide,' Desire had explained in her message. 'My flaws aren't so obvious there. Plus, they don't serve alcohol, so it removes that temptation.'

She was right. Looking around, it was the normal and run-of-the-mill that stood out. As I waited, my head-to-toe black outfit stark against the myriad colours of the café, I was crawling with nerves. In our exchanges, Desire had explained she felt like a ticking timebomb and admitted frankly that she could self-destruct at any moment. I wanted to help, to listen, but I didn't want my mind to be covered in her emotional shrapnel. I couldn't get too involved, not again.

But I just couldn't stop myself.

The bell rang again and I looked up. It was a woman with peroxide blonde hair and dark black roots forming a thick black stripe down the centre of her head. As she scanned the room, I could see thick brown foundation pasted across her face like a mask and mascara smudged around her lashes. As soon my eyes met hers, I knew immediately it was her – the past she'd revealed to me magnified by the pain that had never left her.

I stood up and smiled.

'Desire?' I ventured.

'You must be Chris,' she said as she made her way towards me. I held my hand out but instead she reeled me in for a big hug. Her grip was tight enough that I could feel her collarbone poking into my chest. I was no expert in such matters but it struck me that she could be borderline anorexic.

'So, we finally get to meet,' she said.

'Sorry it's taken so long,' I replied as she released me from her embrace. Her potent perfume clung to my top and danced in my mouth as she took the seat opposite me. Even against the backdrop of the screaming décor, Desire stood out, her presence filling the room and drawing stares from hipster couples sipping their flat whites.

We ordered cappuccinos and batted pleasantries back and forth across the table in an entirely unnecessary game of introductory tennis. I'd already seen into the darkest corners of this woman's soul and her pain needed no introduction because I'd seen it all before.

She had been a resident at Skircoat Lodge as a child and one of the Boss Man's 'favourites'. For two years, from the age of 14, he'd raped and abused her, until she was finally able to leave and live in a hostel. But by then the damage was already done. The years had not been kind to her and she, equally, had not been kind to herself.

You didn't need to know Desire's story to know she was an addict. The roots of the few teeth she had were visible and stained a dark yellow, a less-than-subtle hint that she was in the grip of heroin. As my eyes traced her face, I noticed that the two teeth remaining at the front of her mouth were shaped like thorns, where the bacteria had eroded her cavities into small dark holes.

'I know what you're thinking and you're right. It's not a pretty sight,' she said, stirring her coffee, the teaspoon rhythmically tapping at the side of the cup. I was taken aback by her direct approach.

'Not at all,' I said. 'Who am I to judge?'

Desire knew enough about my life to know I had abused drugs and alcohol to evade the trauma of my life in care. I was there because I cared, regardless of her past or her appearance.

But I was there because she cared too. Like me, she wanted to share her story and her experience in the system so it would never happen again. She'd shared so much already but today she wanted to tell it all.

'From the beginning,' she said. 'I'll start from the beginning.'

Desire was brought up by strict, violent, Catholic parents. For much of her childhood, she lived in fear of sin, judgement – and her father's belt buckle. But as she entered her teenage years, she began to rebel.

'My father beat me whenever I broke the rules,' she said. 'And that was every time I dared to open my mouth.'

But then Desire found out she was pregnant to an older boy who had vanished as quickly as he'd pulled his pants up. For nine months she managed to hide the life growing inside her from her parents, covering her changing body in baggy clothes. But she couldn't keep her secret forever.

At 14 years old, she gave birth to her baby boy. In a park, alone.

'I remember that he fell out face first into the mud,' she said. 'But not much else.'

When her parents found out, they tossed her and the newborn out onto the streets, leaving them to fend for themselves.

'They told me I'd brought unforgivable shame on the family,' she said. 'That I was no longer their daughter.'

It was then that Desire entered the system. Struggling with the trauma of abandonment and grappling with parenthood, she tried to raise her baby with the support of the foster family she had been placed with but she just wasn't ready.

'I made a conscious decision that I no longer wanted to be a teenage mother. I gave the baby up for adoption,' she said.

From this point, her life spiralled out of control. Her placement with the foster family broke down and that was how she found herself in Skircoat Lodge, in the Boss Man's clutches. Her story bore more than a little resemblance to Samantha's story. He'd plied Samantha with treats and alcohol and taken advantage of her while she was under the influence, leaving her to wake up in a pool of her own blood after violently sodomising her. Unlike Samantha though, whose fear had prevented her from speaking up at the time, Desire had raised the alarm.

'I told my social worker what happened,' she said. 'I told the police. But nothing ever happened. In the end, I gave up and tried to move on with my life.'

But it wasn't that easy. As with so many young people in the care system back in the eighties and nineties, no matter how much you tried to escape it, misfortune and the ghosts of your past always caught up with you.

'At 16, the only place I could afford to live was a room in a hostel. I shared with two other girls around my age and three men in their early twenties,' she explained. 'I guess it was inevitable I'd end up with one of them.'

She appeared tough and worldly-wise beyond her years but underneath it all, Desire was still a child. She fell into a relationship with one of the men, who was almost ten years her senior.

'I wasn't allowed to have friends or speak to anyone without his permission,' Desire explained to me, sipping on her fourth cappuccino. 'Everything I did was wrong. He beat me time and again, just like my father did.'

As their relationship progressed, he dug his claws in deeper and exercised his control over Desire. If she refused his demands, he'd use violence or threaten her with abandonment again. At a time when young girls who had been in care were considered worthless pieces of scum, Desire clung on to the only thing she felt she had.

'He would force me to have sex with his friends,' Desire said, tears pricking her eyes. 'If I refused, I'd get his size ten footprint in my face. Or he'd burn me.'

'Burn you?' I asked.

'Oh yeah. The kicks were the lesser punishment, I got used to them,' she said. 'It was the burning that scarred me for life.'

My stomach churned as she told me how he would heat up a knife on the gas fire before placing it on her skin.

'I actually think he enjoyed doing it. He did it whenever he drank, which was every day. It was his favourite way of inflicting pain. But it wasn't the only way,' she said. 'He once beat me up so badly that I was in hospital for two weeks. He sat by my bedside and the moment I came round, he wrapped his hands round my neck and strangled me.'

'Why?' I gasped.

'He didn't want to give me the chance to speak up,' she said. 'As he choked me, he told me I had to tell the police that three Asian men had jumped me.'

'Or what?' I asked.

'What do you think?' she shrugged.

Back then, there was no language for girls like Desire to explain coercive control and gaslighting. Even if there had been, it wouldn't have made any difference. Even if she'd had the words, they'd have been disregarded. Girls like her ended up where they did through their own choices was the common belief – they were where they belonged. Getting what they deserved.

I thought about Yonah, Dardan and Daniel. About how they were treated by the police, social workers and the paper pushers at the Home Office. Attitudes really hadn't changed much at all.

'How did you get away from him?' I asked.

'He got sentenced to ten years for armed robbery,' she said. 'But I didn't get any better at picking my men.'

After escaping her boyfriend, she got involved with another group of men. Like the others before them, they took their pound of flesh. They forced heroin into her arms and made her an addict, a slave to the drug and to them, so they could rape and abuse her as they pleased.

By the time Desire was 28, she had been raped more than 100 times, had suffered ten miscarriages and had four children taken from her by social services. She'd been beaten black and blue so often that she barely remembered what her own, unblemished skin looked like and she was addicted to heroin, glue and aerosols. She had a criminal record as long as her arm and she'd cheated death more times than she cared to admit, sniffing petrol when she had no money and overdosing on cheap heroin.

The light in the café was fading as Desire finished her story.

'I read your book and it made me want to try again,' she said. 'I saw how people had spoken out about the Boss Man and others like him and I wanted to do the same. So I went back to the police station and I filed another complaint.'

'What happened?' I asked, my heart skipping a hopeful beat. *Would she get the break that she deserved?*

'Nothing,' she said. 'Brushed under the carpet again.'

My face must have sunk as low as my heart because Desire leaned over and touched my hand.

'But I'm glad I tried,' she said.

I sat back in my chair and tried to restrain myself from crying, wondering how she managed to remain so calm and collected.

'I haven't cried since I was a child,' she said, reading my mind.

Then she looked up and out. Not into the distance but far, far into her past.

'I'm not even sure I can anymore,' she said faintly. Then she turned and looked me dead in the eye.

'That's what happens when you viscerally die, Chris,' she said.

Her calm delivery sent another wave of emotion washing over me. Here she was, this tired angel, with a spiritual outlook on life, telling me that her experiences had left her devoid of those deepest and most guttural emotions. She's been numb since the first time a hand had been laid upon her.

As we said our goodbyes at the café door, I turned to Desire.

'How do you do it?' I asked.

'Do what?' she asked.

'Keep going, keep positive,' I said.

'Well, what doesn't kill you, and all that jazz,' she replied with a smile, before flicking her peroxide hair over her shoulder and walking away, heels clicking on the concrete as she went.

After meeting Desire, the question was never 'Why did this happen?' or, 'How did this happen?' I already knew the answer to that. The question, for me, was this.

How do we take the abuses and injustices of the past, as well as the mistakes we are still making in the system at present, and use them to effect real change for those in care now and in the future?

Before writing *Damaged*, returning to Halifax was a traumatic experience. Days before I was due to visit, regardless of the occasion, my head would be heavy as lead, my chest tight and I'd wake from dreams of its green hills laced with mist drenched in sweat. The closer I got to the M62, the more my stomach would churn and contract and when I crossed that invisible perimeter surrounding the town, a panic attack would seize my body and force me to pull over until it passed.

But after my story was out there, everything changed. The response from former residents of Skircoat Lodge was overwhelming. Many who had read my book wanted to share their own stories and experiences with me and with the world. Seeing the truth in print had freed them, some had even gone to the police to report the abuse they'd been subjected to.

For the first time I don't feel alone.

I thought it was just me, that it was my fault. Now I know I wasn't to blame.

I'd never told anyone what he did to me. But after reading your book, I did.

Others did not welcome me lifting the lid off the past. But despite the mixed feelings among the former residents' community, and the Facebook page the disgruntled core set up to attack me, I felt a sense of freedom. Of community. There was more than just me and those whose stories had been told in the book. We were not alone. Finally, I could breathe, even if the early morning mist was still polluted with the secrets and lies of those who had caused so much misery to so many.

I understood the anger, the fear of turfing up the past, the shame. I'd felt it all myself, years earlier. That was the reason that I wanted to face those former children of Skircoat Lodge, to address their concerns but also to explain what I hoped to achieve by sharing my story and, by extension, theirs.

I arranged for us to meet in the Murgatroyd Arms on Skircoat Green, next to the old care home, to talk over food and a few drinks before taking a walk past the old grounds, where we could continue our conversations. Forty people in total were invited. Some refused outright, others texted me on the day to say that they couldn't face it – the trauma and anxiety of being so close to the old building would just be too much. I understood wholeheartedly. In the end, only six people attended, two men and four women. It was testament yet again to the destructive nature of a morally and legally corrupt care system.

My appreciation for the bravery of those six people was endless.

The atmosphere was as tense as you might expect as I explained how I'd already started using the book as a springboard for activism, to address historic cases of abuse in care homes and to learn from the mistakes of the past.

'I want us to be a voice for young people in the care system *now*,' I explained.

I wanted our collective pain to have a purpose.

Despite many tears being shed and difficult topics discussed, it was a special afternoon. Our experiences of the past and how they had shaped our lives were poignantly shared by the table of survivors. Although we did not know each other, we were now connected by our souls that were in search of answers, forgiveness and reassurance that the nightmares of Skircoat

Lodge Children's Home would never resurface, and that the mistakes of the past would never be repeated.

The meeting strengthened my resolve to seek justice and support for survivors of Skircoat Lodge. During my visit to Halifax, I had also arranged to meet with the new director of children and young people's services at Calderdale Council, Julie Jenkins. She was aware of Skircoat Lodge's history and the issues the council service had faced over time. Calderdale Council's Children's Services had eventually been deemed inadequate and put in special measures. Even after five years' hard work to address the issues and finally creating an environment where children were 'able to flourish', the service still required improvement in 2015. It took until 2019 for the service to achieve an 'outstanding' rating from Ofsted. But was that really enough?

Yes, improvements had been made. Some of the perpetrators had been sent to jail. One had committed suicide before he could face justice. But knowing some of the monsters that had haunted their dreams had been imprisoned wasn't enough for many of the home's survivors – a whole generation of children who had been let down by the system. To my knowledge and to this date, not one of them has received a public apology for the mass negligence caused by the local council at the time. I don't blame Calderdale Council for the horrific things that went on at Skircoat Lodge. I don't blame any of the councils up and down the country for what happened in homes just like the one I lived in. But I do hold them accountable for ignoring serious allegations of historic sexual abuse, for not setting up support groups for the survivors and for not apologising.

The importance of an apology to those affected cannot be underestimated. One victim, who had been raped and physically abused at the home, told me that an apology from the council would be more beneficial to her than any form of monetary compensation.

'It would mean more to me than winning the lottery,' she told me.

And why? Because it would mean those in power accepted responsibility for what happened and the home's victims could finally stop blaming themselves.

After *Damaged* was published, I received an anonymous message from another survivor, a woman who had buried the sexual abuse she had endured at the hands of the Boss Man for 25 years. Now an adult with two thriving grown-up children, she told me how she'd lived her entire life with mental health issues because of what happened but had never spoken about it because she didn't want anyone to see her as a 'slut' or 'trash'. But after reading the book, she had decided that she could no longer keep her secret and had told her family exactly what had happened to her.

It was in this letter that I learned that new flats had been built on the site of the old care home and had retained its name.

'The home is gone but the building's name and the original sign is still there,' the woman explained. 'I think its disrespectful and the sign should be removed, don't you agree?'

I most certainly did.

To most people it looked like any normal sign but for the children who had resided at Skircoat Lodge Children's Home it was a sign of evil. Once you crossed over that threshold you were entering a world of pain, abuse and fear.

I had raised the issue in my meeting with Julie Jenkins. But to press the issue further, I had to go to the top. So I emailed Halifax MP, Holly Lynch, and asked to meet her to discuss the concerns and needs of the home's survivors. When we met a few weeks later at Portcullis House, facing the Houses of Parliament, it was clear from her age that she had very little personal knowledge of the history of Skircoat Lodge.

Her focus was on the future of the town and not on its past. But despite her personal political goals, she was still willing to listen and understand the impact the sign was having on a number of her constituents. At the end of our meeting she promised to do all within her power to have the sign removed. Contrary to my experience with most politicians, Holly stuck to her word and went straight to work, doing her research and making the right calls.

Around the same time, I received a message from a former police detective in Halifax. He claimed to have been involved in Operation Screen, the investigation into abuse at Skircoat Lodge in 1980s. Working in the force, he'd had to take many runaways back to the home and he'd heard all the rumours about the 'bad things' that went on there. In his message, he admitted that complaints were dismissed as bad blood but he said that once, while working as a detective, he saw a young resident – a girl of around nine years old – climb onto some furniture in her nightie while he was waiting to interview someone.

'She was not wearing any knickers. I wish I had said something then and I will always regret it,' he said. 'I'd always thought the boss there was sound, until the court case, that is.'

Years later, it emerged that the Boss Man had enforced a strict policy banning the girls at the home from wearing knickers.

I was enraged by his impunity. It was as if he wanted absolution for his part in what happened – because by turning a blind eye he'd made himself compliant. I knew first-hand from what I had seen as a professional in the sector how easy it could be to look away from evidence of mistreatment and abuse. To avert your gaze to maintain your job security and healthy salary, as well as avoiding a mountain of paperwork.

In some ways, it was the same crossroads that I had faced. Abandoning the young people in my care in favour of profit and a cushy lifestyle. But I hadn't.

Because how could you?

Ultimately, Halifax MP Holly Lynch's attempt to remove Skircoat Lodge's sign was unsuccessful and it's still there today. But it's hardly surprising. We live in a world where a former police officer seeks absolution for missed chances to help vulnerable children, where an MP – now our prime minister, Boris Johnson – says in a radio interview that funds spent investigating historic child abuse were money that had been 'spaffed up the wall' (a shockingly poor choice of words, given the subject matter) and where young people are still abused at the hands of power and no one even bats an eyelid.

In the wake of Boris Johnson's comments, Louise Haigh, the then-shadow policing minister, said his remarks were insulting to survivors of abuse. And she was right, it was a kick in the teeth for thousands of victims who were relying on the government to take up their cases with the Crown Prosecution Service.

'Could you look the victims in the eye and tell them investigating and bringing to justice those who abused them, as children, is a waste of money?' she said, in a message aimed at Johnson.

The whole incident reinforced something that my visit to Halifax had made clearer than ever. The world I inhabited was split into two groups: those who would speak up and fight both for those who had been abused in care homes as children *and* young people currently in our care system, and those that wouldn't.

Despite the failure of the campaign to remove the Skircoat Lodge sign, Holly's good intent was a glimmer of hope. She was a young politician who *was* willing to stand up for care kids. We just need more like her. It is the survivors of historic child abuse in the British care system, with their lived experience, together with professionals working in the care sector and politicians and others in positions of power and authority who can take the mistakes of the past and ensure that they are not repeated, and make sure that children in care are given the help, support and protection that they need.

If we don't do this, they will become victims facing a life sentence and a miscarriage of dreams. Many will end up like Desire, in a cycle of self-destruction. But if we do – if we empower and protect those in the system and support care leavers effectively – we can pave the way for a far brighter future and amazing things can happen.

CHAPTER TEN

Surviving the System

Isabella

I'D JUST FINISHED a workshop at a community centre when she approached me. Alongside campaigning and getting stuck into the politics of the issues affecting children in care, I'd started delivering sessions to groups of care leavers and other professionals, where I shared my own experiences and tried my best to provide them with some tools to help them thrive after leaving the system.

I'd wrapped up my talk by highlighting how, if the foundations of a system were cracked from the beginning, then the inevitable would happen – everything would crumble, eventually.

To illustrate, I used the Leaning Tower of Pisa as an example.

'The tower started to lean during construction because the soft ground beneath it could not support the structure's weight,' I explained. 'It worsened as the project progressed and the builders could all see it leaning, but they ignored it.'

'But it's still standing, isn't it?' a small voice piped up.

'You're right,' I nodded, as I tried to pick the owner of the voice out from the crowd. 'But it's a building that can't be properly used. It's not fit for its intended purpose . . . '

The voice from the crowd emerged again. 'Like the care system,' it said.

'Exactly,' I said. 'This is why we need to address the issues in the system now. We can see them. As care leavers and professionals we know the ramifications. We need to use our voices and experience to get those in power to address the problems and make the system fit for purpose.'

As my talk ended and the audience began to file out, I noticed a figure lingering near her seat and looking at me, as if she wanted to come and chat, but wasn't sure if she should. I smiled and waved her over.

Isabella was 18 and studying law. In comparison to some of the other children in the room whose stories I already knew, she'd come into care relatively late. A volatile relationship with her mum had created a toxic environment at home. When they clashed, as parents and teenagers almost always do, her mum would lash out with her fists rather than words and Isabella would fight back. The contours of the bruises on her face told her story for all the world to see but it was her grandma who spoke up. Living her whole life on a deprived council estate, Isabella's grandma knew a thing or two about keeping young people safe.

'She'd have taken me in herself, if she wasn't too old for the drama,' Isabella explained. 'So she called the local authorities instead because she knew I never would.'

'Were you angry at her?' I asked.

'No, not in the end,' she said. 'My grandma just wanted to protect me – and rescue my mum too.'

'Rescue her from what?' I asked.

'Desolation. Her own unhappiness was pushing her to self-destruct,' she said.

'And she was taking you with her,' I said, understanding the predicament Isabella's grandmother would have faced.

Of course, the local authority didn't swoop in like super-heroes to help Isabella. At 16 and out of the risky environment of her home, she was pretty low down the priority list. In fact, she ended up homeless and sofa surfing at the homes of friends and acquaintances for 16 months until the authorities finally stepped up and placed her in supported accommodation.

Fortunately for Isabella, that blip was the worst of her experience in care. The house she was placed in was clean, safe and had a supportive staff team that was on hand 24 hours a day to help its residents.

'My dad left us when I was six. He just upped and left one morning, never to be seen again,' she said. 'So I'd never really known living like a family. But that's how it felt in the house. The staff, my housemates were my family.'

Unlike so many others in the care system, ripped from their home area and placed hundreds of miles away from all that they knew, her accommodation was only a short bus ride from the estate she'd grown up on so she stayed in touch with old friends too. Many of her peers were in similar positions, warring with parents who had been broken by poverty, addiction or abuse. Isabella was the only one in care but none of them went to school. As for finding work, well, the opportunities were limited for young people coming off the estate.

'We were bored,' she shrugged. 'Hanging around the streets together was all we could do. We didn't even have a community centre anymore.'

Isabella barely remembered the community centre. It was something of a mirage in her mind from her childhood. Tory budget cuts had run it into the ground. Residents kept it going as long as they could, their graft and passion a defibrillator for the heart of the estate, but in the end they had to call it.

Without a hub to congregate at, the community spirit died and desolation rolled across the estate, a heavy cloud enveloping any glimmers of hope. Even the youth workers who had once tirelessly patrolled the area vanished in the fog of despair. Everything was grey, from the concrete slabs of the once-vibrant courtyard to the tower blocks that dwarfed the teenagers ricocheting around the fractured stone paths and dark alleyways.

The only colour Isabella remembered from the estate was the bright red coat of the postman, who arrived with his bag bulging every Tuesday morning.

'He stood out like a single rose in a field of weeds,' she recalled fondly. 'He'd wave and say a cheery "hello". I always wondered if he was bringing good news to someone, somewhere on the estate. I know better now.'

I nodded. We both knew the bag was more likely to be filled with final payment demands, bills and court summons.

During the day, the estate was a desert, devoid of life. The majority of its residents were too old to move away and too scared to venture outside so they hibernated in their shoebox-sized flats. But it came alive when night fell, vibrating with the cacophonous sound of juvenility. Drum and base, grime and drill, Skepta to Dave. The music resonated around the estate, oscillating back and forth, bouncing off the walls, alarming older residents and emboldening the youths that gathered to talk, deal and settle disputes.

Evidence of gang life was evident in all corners of the estate but the elders who'd fostered a community years earlier were too afraid and worn down to challenge the new powers in play. Isabella saw it all but steered clear of trouble.

'Weren't you scared?' I asked. 'You must have seen some bad things?'

'This was our ends,' she shrugged. 'That's how we lived.'

'You're very mature for your age,' I said.

'I had to grow up quick, Chris,' she replied. 'I didn't want to fall into the slums and become a cliché.'

After years of seeing the system beat the hope out of so many young people, after witnessing so many negative outcomes for kids in care and hearing so many dysfunctional stories, finally hearing someone being so proudly positive lifted a weight off my shoulders that I didn't realise I'd been carrying.

Isabella had it on the nose but of course everything depends on the individual and the tools they have to survive. That is what made all the difference. Maybe part of it was her own mindset, her unwillingness to be a victim, but she had also been well-equipped by the system.

It had done its job, for once.

The system had supported her properly until she turned 18, when it finally wished her good luck and gently closed its doors, rather than booting her unceremoniously off a cliff edge with no parachute like it did to most. She was fully independent and juggling full-time education with a raft of part-time jobs.

'I get up at 5am every day and go to my cleaning job at the local hospital,' she said, as she explained how she fitted it all in. 'From there I go straight to college until 3pm.'

Inspired by those who had supported her and driven to help young people like her to better understand their rights, she was studying law.

'After college I go to another cleaning job at some offices close to where I study,' she said. 'Then I get home around 7pm, make dinner, do my homework and get ready to start all over again the next day.'

'Wow,' I said. 'So your weekends are your own, surely?'

'Are they hell!' she snorted. 'Two cleaning jobs doesn't pay the bills and buy books for school.'

'You have another job?' I gasped, concerns for her wellbeing bubbling inside.

'I just work in a bar at the weekend,' she said. 'I don't really have much time for socialising.'

'Or resting,' I said.

'What choice do I have?' she replied. 'I can't cry about it. My future, my problem.'

I admired the ownership of her situation, her approach.

'I can look at my life as a scab or a scar,' she said.

'What do you mean?' I asked, brow furrowed.

'There's a sense of relief you get when you pick a scab, isn't there? It hurts at first, then it becomes oddly pleasurable,' she said. 'It makes you feel comfortable but if you keep picking the scab, the wound never really goes away.'

'OK,' I nodded, eager to see where she was going with the metaphor.

'On the other hand, if you fight the urge and leave it to heal, you're left with a scar. A reminder of the past without the distraction of picking away at an old scab.'

She didn't want to miss her chance and end up picking away and thinking 'what if?' – but she didn't want to forget where she'd come from either. Her situation wasn't the consequence of anything she'd done but she accepted where she was.

She just didn't see the point of picking away at the wound.

She refused to see herself as a victim.

But I knew that she was. She was a victim of our failed system.

It's just that, somehow, she was managing to forge herself a path out of the mess the system had left her in. She knew her circumstances were unfortunate. She knew that it shouldn't be like this but she was also well aware that hundreds – even thousands – of young people had it far worse than her.

'If I don't do this now, what prospects do I have? What chance do *I* have without qualifications?' she said. 'I have to work so I can study. There's no financial support for kids like me to focus just on our education.'

She was right. Without the cushion of the support from a parent or guardian, there was nothing. There were no loans because there was no one to back them. They could only rely on their own graft.

'Kids from council estates don't get to choose how to live, we get told,' she said.

It took a moment for the meaning of her words to sink in.

She believed her path was predetermined.

The routes for kids like her – from care or poor backgrounds – were already mapped out for them. They could fall into the same cycle that brought them to this point, the self-fulfilling prophecy of poverty. Or fight with every ounce of their being to get out.

They didn't have the same options as middle-class kids, or those with stable family lives. They didn't have the luxury of choice. The iniquity of the system left a bitter taste in my mouth.

But Isabella was more philosophical. She had friends at college who went home to a family and lived a normal teenage life. But she wasn't jealous or bitter, she accepted her circumstances as a test of strength.

She placed her chin on the top of her hand and stared thoughtfully.

'I'm not a religious person as such but—' then she broke off suddenly, '—I don't go to church because I have to work,' she smiled. 'But I believe that God has bigger plans for me,' she said.

Suddenly, Lemn Sissay's documentary about care leavers *Superkids*[1] came into my mind. He'd called to end the misconception of care kids as broken goods and hailed them instead as superheroes. He'd looked at popular fictional characters who had been displaced from their birth families – Superman, Harry Potter and Spider-Man, to name a few – and spoken of how their journeys had given them powers that other kids didn't have.

'What do you reckon your superhero name would be?' I asked Isabella, after telling her about the series.

'Me? I'd be Spectacular Optimism,' she said, before laughing from the pit of her stomach. I couldn't help but join in with her.

'It's perfect,' I said.

She might not be able to fly or cast spells but her superpowers were her tenacity, her ability to keep going and her ability to stay optimistic, no matter what.

As our conversation drew to a close, Isabella looked at me. It was clear I was inspired by her story but everything I had seen of the system made me worry for her future. My concern must have been as obvious as my admiration.

'Chris,' she said. 'My road might not be smooth but I'm adaptable. I can navigate all surfaces. I'll be OK.'

---

[1] www.channel4.com/programmes/superkids-breaking-away-from-care

'I know you will be,' I said.

And for the first time since entering the world of semi-independent care, I think I actually meant it.

Meeting Isabella had a profound impact on me. After two years of watching hope being snuffed out for so many kids who had passed through my care, after seeing the stories of so many victims of historic abuse in care homes still being swept until the carpet, like a dirty secret, I was beginning to feel the fight drain out of me. I was weighed down by a mountain of seemingly unresolvable problems, stooping under the pressure, like that rose bush in my garden. I knew it was bad because Androulla kept asking if I was OK, eyeing me like I looked at the withered leaves of the plant in winter, wondering if it would ever manage to bloom again.

Isabella was a beacon of hope. The proof I needed to see that – given the right support – care leavers *could* thrive. Despite her initial shyness, her observation about the Leaning Tower of Pisa was almost defiant. It was still standing.

She was still standing.

I wasn't fighting a fruitless battle. There was hope. Meeting her also made me realise that I needed to fight for changes that would allow care kids to do much more than merely survive. My mission had to be for more than just the bare minimum. I needed to find a new way that would help them reach their potential.

I didn't want to hear, 'They've done well, considering.' I wanted to hear people saying, 'What an exceptional individual'

– no qualifiers or caveats. Isabella reinvigorated my mission and I understood the impact her story could have on other care leavers.

You see, as well as support, our kids in care need to feel like they are seen as humans with value, as equals. Seeing positive role models in the mainstream – out there in society, speaking unashamedly of coming through the care system – is hugely important. If you don't see yourself in society, it's easy to believe you're not a part of it – or a worthwhile one, at least. That's why we need more voices like Isabella and me, like Lemn Sissay, Fatima Whitbread and Neil Morrissey, to be examples of what might be possible.

That said, inspiration will only get care kids so far. Full support is only offered by the care system up to the age of 18. It does offer some external support for care leavers up until the age of 25 but not enough. It's limited and doesn't address the most pressing issues care leavers face.

Most young people want nothing more than to be fully independent and make a life for themselves, like Isabella. To do that, education is vital, yet there is no support that allows care leavers to focus on their studies without having to work to maintain their access to education.

In our conversation, Isabella and I agreed that no young person should be forced to work to survive. Having a part-time job alongside college could be a good thing for your life skills and CV but as a young adult, your education should not be reliant on you holding down multiple unskilled jobs that pay below minimum wage.

So many young people leaving the care system fail in their ambitions because of this issue. They have to put paying bills and eating before learning. A report published in July 2020 highlighted that just 13 per cent of care leavers had progressed to higher education by 2018/19, compared to 43 per cent of all other pupils.[2] Those who do go to college are far more likely to drop out than their peers.

That's what segregates them from kids from 'normal' backgrounds. 'Normal' kids don't have to make the choice between surviving and thriving. They have the necessary support in place that allows them to do the latter. In an ideal world, Isabella would be living at home with her mum, not having to worry about the electric being switched off, not having to work three jobs to pay her rent. She'd be able to focus on her studies and maybe even end up going to university.

But kids in the care system have come from – or at least ended up in – less than ideal situations. Without the right kind of support, despite their ambitions, hopes and dreams, they never get to where they want to be.

Where they have every right to be.

I am certain that Isabella's stoic resilience will give her ability to push through the challenges but not everyone has that resilience naturally. What about those who need a little extra help?

---

[2] explore-education-statistics.service.gov.uk/find-statistics/widening-participation-in-higher-education This statistic refers to pupils who were looked after continuously for 12 months or more at 31 March 2015.

Young people leaving the care sector have the ability to learn like anyone else. So why doesn't the government work harder to ensure they have the same opportunities as their peers to develop skills and grow as people? Attitudes and austerity ingrained in society as a result of more than a decade of Conservative leadership have done a fine job of 'othering' care kids, conjuring up an image of lawless, lazy wasters and drains on society.

The reality really couldn't be further from the truth.

Isabella had nothing but praise for her experience in care, yet she recognised it was not usual. The reality is, with better support structures, the care system would be churning out Isabellas ten to the dozen. But, in the main, instead of investing in the futures of young people in care in this country, the state simply hurls them through a broken and often corrupt system, pushing them ever closer to the exit doors as they near their eighteenth birthday. Towards the care cliff that awaits them outside.

CHAPTER ELEVEN

The Care Cliff

Alex

THE POLLUTED MIST SPREAD across the ocean that lay in front of him, carrying with it the pungent smell of rot. A tinny rendition of 'Nothing Else Matters' by Metallica played from his phone as he slowly and methodically removed his clothes, folding each item and leaving them in a neat pile beside a rock.

He didn't want to leave that burden to whoever found them.

After he was gone.

It was typical of Alex. Always thinking of others. Even in his last moments, he was worried about his actions causing inconvenience to someone else. Once he was naked, he turned to the dark expanse of water, stretching as far as his eye could see, and took a deep breath. Looking down, he began to walk forward, stepping gingerly over the pebbles to avoid the ones that looked sharp and dangerous.

Ironic, he thought.

But this was *his* end and he was in control. He wanted it to be as smooth and painless as possible. Not like the years he'd endured prior to this moment. A lifetime of pain inflicted by matters entirely outside his control. He'd been in danger his whole life. This was the consequence of the actions of those who had been meant to care for and protect him – his mother, his social workers, the state. None of them had fulfilled their duty to him.

As he reached the water he dipped his left foot in and shuddered.

It was freezing. Far colder than anything his body was prepared for. But he gritted his teeth and persevered, submerging his right foot and moving forward until the icy blackness engulfed his legs, his waist, his torso . . .

By now his teeth had unclenched and were chattering like the wind-up ones you'd find in a joke shop. His brain was frantically signalling his nervous system, raising the alarm that his body needed to find a way to warm up. But it didn't respond. It had given up fighting.

His chattering teeth only fell silent as his head disappeared into the water. The deeper he sank, the smaller the oxygen rings rising from his lips became. As the last circles of life bubbled on the surface, expanding outwards until they vanished into the gentle waves rippling steadily on, silence prevailed.

That was it.

He was gone.

I stood open-mouthed and heart racing as the silence wrapped itself around me. The quiet devastation of the scene hypnotised me, until his words snapped me back into reality.

'It's always the same,' Alex said. 'I can see myself. It's all in the third person and I'm the narrator of my own death, like David Attenborough in a wildlife documentary.'

'And that's the recurring dream you have about your suicide?' I confirmed.

'Yeah. But it feels so real,' he said, looking down at the faint silver scars on his wrists. 'I never had the balls to actually do it. But if I *was* going to do it, that's how I would do it.'

I'd only met Alex a few times. I had set up my own company, Phoenix Caring, to work as a consultant to care provisions looking after young people. He was 21 and living in supported accommodation for care leavers, which was run by a charity that I had been doing youth outreach for. The law says that every child in care should be supported until the age of 25, the degree to which depending on their circumstances. For young care leavers not classed as 'vulnerable' or 'at risk' local authorities are simply obligated to appoint a personal advisor to provide guidance on things like finance, education and housing. It's advice rather than tangible support, which is why so many young care leavers turn to charities for help.

Alex had spent the best part of his childhood living in poverty, moving from home to home and shelter to refuge house. He had no idea who his dad was because his mother was a drug addict and had been too high to remember. Which was maybe for the best because she had a propensity for dangerous men who drank too much and lashed out with their fists.

'I wouldn't recognise Mum without a black eye or a face full of foundation to hide her bruises,' he said. 'I can't remember a time when her face wasn't scarred. But she *was* beautiful underneath all the makeup. That's how I remember her.'

She'd accidentally overdosed on heroin when Alex was 16 so memories were all he had, even if they weren't conventional ones. They were the type that those of us who'd experienced even a flicker of a stable family life couldn't even begin to comprehend.

'I remember one night when we were homeless, when Mum and I were living on the Strand, there was a huge storm,' he said, eyes wide with excitement. 'The lightning reflected on the Thames and the whole place lit up like a laser show and the thunder echoed under the bridges. It was magical, like a rock concert or something.'

Alex seemed to be able to find beauty in the darkest of places. I think it was because he'd always had to. With no other family and unable to fend for himself, he had been taken into care by the local authorities, who became his corporate parent.

'I still find it mad that all my life I was living in danger. My mum was an addict and the men in her life were violent. I was at risk from the moment I was born but the authorities did nothing,' he shrugged. 'They didn't give a shit about me then but as soon as my mum died, they wanted to help.'

'Why do you think that was?' I asked.

'Because that's how it works. My mum was very good at pretending things were all fine and dandy, especially in front of professionals. Every time a social worker rocked up, Mum would cover her face in thick, cheap makeup and put on this spectacle,' he said, then he stopped, looked at me and raised an eyebrow. 'She would have made a good actress, you know,' he added, a hint of pride in his voice.

There must have been an artistic streak running through the family. When I first started working with him, Alex was studying art at college and making music at night. He was incredibly talented and lit up when he spoke of his creative endeavours. The first time I met him, he was wearing a pair of colourful jeans that looked like they could've been designed by Alexander McQueen.

'Where did you get your jeans from?' I asked inquisitively.

'These are just cheap Primark jeans that I ripped here and there, then dyed orange and green,' he said. 'Not bad, eh?'

'They look designer,' I marvelled.

'You can make anything look a million dollars if you try,' he said.

Even though I didn't work with Alex for long, it was obvious that creativity was his refuge. He had suffered throughout his youth with severe mental health issues as a result of the things he had seen growing up.

'I'd often find Mum lying unconscious with a needle in her arm,' he explained. 'It was the norm. So was seeing men beating her up and, you know . . .'

He trailed off but I knew what he was insinuating. I'd read in his notes how, on more than one occasion, he'd witnessed men violently raping his mum. That kind of trauma would inevitably have a psychological effect on your life.

How could it not?

As a child, Alex had been supported by Child and Adolescent Mental Health Services, or CAMHS, but as a young adult he'd been reluctant to engage with any of the services they offered. Endless paperwork and useless referrals pinging back and forth simply to deliver the most basic support had worn him down. So, when he was 17, they discharged him.

Shortly after that, he turned 18 and he was one of the unlucky ones in the housing lottery. He didn't get a place on the social housing list so he had to find somewhere else to live. There were just too many young people in need and not enough places made available for them.

If it hadn't been for the charity I was working with, God knows where he might have ended up. Alex was edging ever closer to the point where support would no longer be available when the charity had agreed to house him in their supported accommodation, following an assessment by an Association for Children's Mental Health (ACMH) social worker and ACMH nurse. Although Alex was capable of being fully independent in many ways, he still had underlying issues that needed to be dealt with. He wasn't ready to be left without any support.

It was a discussion of his ongoing mental health issues that had led to Alex describing his vivid suicide dream to me. He'd also told me about a time, when he was 17, that he'd slit his wrists and been admitted into a psychiatric ward. He was there for just three weeks before he was discharged back to the bedsit he'd ended up in at 16, with no social worker or other professional to support him. Since he was not on the at risk register, he'd flown under the radar.

'I had no intention of killing myself,' he said. 'I just wanted to get out of that fucking shithole. Going into hospital was like going on holiday.'

'How do you mean?' I probed.

'I had my meals made for me. It was clean and I had some fucking company. Apart from all the assessment shit it was serene. I just painted and slept all day.'

While he explained his rationale to me, my stomach contorted as I absorbed the implications. Food, shelter, safety and company. That was all he wanted. Such basic needs. All denied to a child.

You see, at 17, Alex was still a *child* in the eyes of the law, a child who had been forced, by the failings of the state and our care system, to live in conditions so unbearable that he would physically harm himself to escape them, even just for a short time. There had been no one for him to turn to, to help him sort out his accommodation situation. No one to provide him with the support he needed. Hurting himself was the only way to get the attention of the authorities.

I dreaded to think what might have happened if the charity hadn't stepped in. Would he have reached a point when he was ready to go to the watery grave in his dreams?

Thankfully, the charity had moved Alex into a building with seven other young people, all from similar backgrounds. He was in a good place. He had a home in London, his hometown, a place in college doing something he loved. Something he was *good* at. As our conversations progressed, I saw a young man who, with a little support, could really thrive.

Although Alex spoke honestly about his darker thoughts, most of our conversations were positive. He wanted very little in life and his dreams were reachable. Making music, producing, these were the things that made him feel alive and he was doing them. Whenever he said he felt like he wasn't getting anywhere because of his background, I reminded him of how many of his idols came from nothing. When he felt like giving up, I tried to get him to consider his goals.

'It's not about reaching the top of a mountain,' I said. 'It's the small steps to get there.'

'What do you mean?' he asked.

'You don't just get up and climb Mount Everest,' I replied. 'It takes years to prepare. Most people don't make it to the summit – but they achieve a hell of a lot trying to. You don't get anywhere without hard work and sacrifice.'

'What do you mean by sacrifice?' he asked.

'The choices you make,' I explained. 'Nothing happens without choosing to give certain things up. You chose to avoid joining a gang so you could go to college and study. People expected you to end up involved in crime, but you didn't, you made a choice.'

'But won't people always see me as someone who should be in a gang?' he asked.

'Why do you say that?' I asked.

Alex paused for a minute, as if he was trying to find the words to explain what was going on in his mind.

'OK, let me ask you a question,' he said, finally.

'Go on,' I said.

'Does a lab rat live better than a sewer rat?' he asked.

I paused for a minute to consider the options.

'I think they both live a crap life,' I shrugged.

'Exactly,' he replied. 'The lab rat is treated like shit yet it lives in luxury. Sewer rats live in shit and they are treated like shit. Nothing changes, it's shit no matter what. So is it better to be a sewer rat, than a lab rat?'

I couldn't answer the question but I understood it. Even if they rise out of the sewers or escape the labs, they're still rats. Society has labelled them vermin and that's all they know from birth.

'Now imagine being a black teenager with a junkie mum and trying to be anything but a rat,' he finished.

But I wanted him to be able to see what he considered to be his weakness – his struggle through life and the place he had come from – as a strength.

'How society views you is wrong; it underestimates you. Everything you have been through makes you stronger than most,' I said. 'The things that "normal" kids do, you have done after sleeping in a shed for two weeks in winter. You have already been through, seen and experienced so much more than other people of your age, and you can use that to get yourself where you want to be.'

I'd planted the seed. But it was Alex who had to nourish it.

I watched as he took everything in. Then he spoke.

'You know what, Chris, I'd rather try to climb the mountain and fail, than give up,' he said.

I nodded in agreement and a thoughtful silence, laden with mutual respect, fell between us. When that happened, I knew I was leaving Alex in a good place.

But it didn't last.

How could it?

Alex and his other housemates had all reached the end of the line when it came to formal provisions from the care sector. Their time with the charity was limited too.

It wasn't a permanent solution.

It was a stay of execution.

There was a conveyor belt of young people waiting to take his room, all with aspirations like his that were set to be shattered by austerity and a lack of empathy in the system.

As the deadline for his departure loomed, I watched the pressure of trying to find affordable housing in London weigh him down. We did everything we could to help him, aware of the ticking clock hanging over him, but it was near impossible to find anything to rent for less than £1,200 a month and those you could weren't even fit for the rats that came with the tenancy.

Reliant on universal credit and housing benefit, like so many of his care-experienced peers, Alex was faced with a choice of moving out of London and away from everything he knew or taking on a minimum-wage job and trying to scrape enough together to pay for a hovel. I sat with him as he weighed up his options.

'I lived on the streets before so I'm not scared to go back there,' he shrugged, 'and if it's the only alternative to leaving the city, what other choices do I have?'

'But surely living in a house in Birmingham is better than sleeping on the streets in London?' I said.

'What life do I have there though, Chris?' he asked. 'I don't have much here but I have worked so hard for it. Why should I give it up?'

I understood his point but I knew the state didn't.

The elites who had the power to remove this decision from care leavers' shoulders looked down their noses and dismissed their pleas.

The audacity! These children should be grateful to have a roof over their heads anywhere!

Alex didn't give up without a fight. He got himself a night job at Aldi and found a single room in a shared house on the outskirts of London. It was miles away from his friends and college.

But it was London, at least.

Despite all his efforts, it wasn't enough. After he moved out of the charity's housing I didn't see him again but we kept in touch by messaging every now and again.

Usually he was upset, or even in a state of distress. It didn't take long before he was behind on his college work and his rent. He was too tired to make his classes. The journey now took him two hours, instead of 40 minutes, and he wasn't earning enough on the shifts he could get to pay for his room, bills, food, travel *and* college.

In the end, after applying to countless other housing associations and charities, he was moved to accommodation nearly 150 miles away in Wolverhampton.

It was his only option.

His world fell apart and I watched as his mental health began to unravel, unable to offer anything more than supportive words or a listening ear.

'I've lost my entire childhood. Nothing feels real anymore. I don't know who I am or what my purpose is,' he messaged one day. 'The authorities have ruined my life.'

'Do you want to talk about it?' I replied. 'I'm here, you know.'

I never heard from Alex again.

Alex didn't choose to be brought into this world by a drug addict. It wasn't his fault he was beaten just for crying when he was hungry. It wasn't his fault he didn't have any family to fall back on in hard times. It wasn't his fault that he dropped out of college and fell behind on rent.

But the way our government treats young people like him, you'd think it was. Some suggest that the poor outcomes that care leavers experience are inevitable, that they end up in care as children because of circumstances beyond their control, but then stay stuck in a cycle of poor choices. That's when local authorities and the government start laying blame at their feet.

Take, for example, refusing to move hundreds of miles from their hometowns to accommodation in a safer area, in favour of staying local and living in a hostel with drug addicts and criminals. It might look like a poor choice on paper, but to kids in care their local area, the people they know and the services they access are the only safety and security they have known. They have often lived in deprivation and danger before and the fear of isolation and being catapulted to live in a place where they have nothing and know no one is far more frightening.

Is that 'poor choice' really their fault, or is it simply a hand dealt by a system that isn't meeting the needs of the people it is meant to support?

In reality, poor outcomes are only inevitable within the boundaries of our failing and broken care system. I have no doubt that given the right support, Alex would have completed his college course and got a full-time job that paid above minimum wage, allowing him to pay rent, feed himself and build a life. Like Isabella, he had to choose between working to survive or studying to find a way to thrive. Unlike Isabella, despite all his best efforts, he had to do what he needed to in order to survive. This isn't a choice any young person should have to make.

But it's one that thousands are forced to make every day.

Make no mistake, this is the fault of the system. The consequence of the state's attitude to the needs of young people in care. Right now, once you pass the age of 18 in the care sector, you are on borrowed time. The law may say that every child in care should be supported until the age of 25, but the support that's available dwindles the older you get. As a young person in care, you will eventually reach a point where you have exhausted all the help that is available to you.

After that you fall off the edge of a care cliff. You're on your own.

The 'care cliff' is the phrase that charities and organisations supporting care-experienced children and young people use to describe the point when, on turning 18, many young people – whether from the UK like Alex, Daniel and Isabella or asylum seekers like Yonah and Dardan – are unceremoniously ejected from the care system, forced to move out of their home and make independent living arrangements, even if they aren't ready or able to do so.

In some cases, this can happen overnight and young people can end up living in unsuitable accommodation, like the cheap B&Bs and dirty bedsits that are within their budget – if indeed they can afford anything at all.

If they can't, they end up on the streets.

Every council across the country is overwhelmed with caseloads of young people becoming homeless. Young people can be 'nominated' for social housing - that is put forward by a local authority or housing charity for a house – but there is finite supply of social housing that has to be distributed to people across the country. Charities like the one that supported Alex – who provide a stop gap for some care leavers after the age of 18, are only given a small percentage of nominations for social housing.

In 2020, at the start of the pandemic, I worked with one housing charity that had 60 young people all teetering at the edge of the 'care cliff'. As part of my consultancy work, I had to help them decide who, from that 60, to nominate for social housing.

Can you imagine having to make those decisions?

I had worked with many of the young people. Each had their own unique story, their own needs and ongoing issues. The one thing they all had in common was that they needed the safety and stability of a place to live. *A home.*

In my eyes, every single one of them was eligible and deserving.

But the charity only had 14 nominations.

Only 14 people out of 60 in their care would get somewhere to live. The rest – 46 in total – would have to find alternative accommodation within their price range, all by themselves.

If we think it's bad now, without sufficient funding from central government, it's only going to get worse. The 'care cliff' is a relatively new term but not a new phenomenon. It existed when I was in care too. But the need for a term that encompasses the experience of being a child cast out into the world with no safety net has grown exponentially as the numbers of children in care have grown and the budgets available to support them have shrunk.

In November 2020, I supported a campaign calling on the government to end the 'care cliff', which was led by Become, a national charity for children. They encouraged people to tweet a photo of themselves at 18 with the hashtag #WhenIWas18 and a line about what they were doing at the point when our current system would have pulled the rug of support. The campaign exploded. The care-experienced community was coming together with people who wanted to fight to support those currently in or leaving care and it felt like an incredible turning point. I spend hours scrolling through the tweets, recognising myself and so many young people I had supported in the experiences of others. Search on Twitter now and you will see messages from all over the UK – someone who was given a cheque for a few hundred quid after turning 18 and sent on their way, with no life skills, no support and no back up. A 16-year-old living in a bedsit with addicts, with no furniture and stealing from bins. The stories were shocking, but not unfamiliar.

The campaign encouraged me to revisit my own experience of leaving care. When I was 15, my social worker – who had always been great with me – came round and told me that she wouldn't be around for much longer and that I needed to start thinking about how I was going to survive independently. In a way, I didn't believe her but on my sixteenth birthday, sure enough, everyone disappeared, along with the support they had been giving me.

I was alone, isolated and had no idea what to do. In the end, I joined the army. I made it through the recruitment process and ended up stationed in Scotland but I only lasted six weeks. I didn't want to be a soldier, I just wanted what all young people want. What Alex had wanted when he cut his own wrists.

Food, shelter, safety and company.

Life at home, with Viv abusing and gaslighting my mum, had become unbearable to watch and anything seemed better than going back there. When the army didn't work out, I turned to life on the streets. Between my sixteenth and eighteenth birthday, my life was a total void; I was teetering on the precipice before I eventually went over the edge. I think it was my survival instincts that saved me, that and my short stint as a professional boxer. Getting in the gym and gaining some discipline gave me some kind of focus again. I know others that weren't so lucky. You see, when you fall off that care cliff, you either learn to fly or you hit the ground and die – because there is no safety net. No in-between outcome.

This should never have been the case back then. But it certainly should not still be the case now.

Twenty years on, young people are still tumbling over the edge of the same cliff edge I did. And it should never have taken a global crisis – unlike one ever seen in our lifetime – for our government to finally plunge deep into its pockets to find funding for the 'Everyone In' scheme, which gave councils £3.2m to help provide those living on the streets with emergency accommodation, finally breaking out a safety net that's always been there at their disposal.

CHAPTER TWELVE
Tipping Point

SO MUCH OF MY life had been an unpredictable whirlwind that I'd become used to the chaos, spinning through whatever life threw at me and spiralling in my own mind as my trauma pushed my mental health to the precipice. But I was always anchored firmly to the ground by Androulla.

As the years had passed, she'd accepted this as just who I was. Instead of fighting to 'fix' me, she laid the solid foundations I needed to stop me from spinning off my tether and past the point of no return. She was my rock and the reason I was able to take the chaos and turn it into something positive. But towards the end of 2020, something kept tugging on that thread to my sanity, its fibres fraying and pinging one by one as I grappled to ground myself.

Something big was coming. I could feel it.

In December 2019, I'd hit the big 4-0. Maybe that was it? We'd celebrated with a big party – friends and family came from all over to dance, drink, hug and share stories about what we'd all been up to. Even my sister Donna came – all the way from Australia. I hadn't seen her for five years so it had been an extra special gift. But despite all the joy and celebration, I felt sick, the same way I had every year in the run-up to my thirty-sixth birthday. My dad had died when he was 36, his mother at 35 and I'd always wondered if there was a family curse that was coming for me. Donna shared my fear as well. But even though I 'made it' every year and the knot of anxiety loosened a little, another knot tightened.

Guilt.

How had I lived longer than my own father did?

He never made it to 40. Never had reason to get the family together to celebrate.

Why do I deserve this and he didn't? I thought.

Each year, I felt more and more pressure to make something of myself and do something with the years I'd been gifted that my dad had never had. At my party I was surrounded by so much love and support, people congratulating me on what I'd achieved so far and hyping me up about what was to come. But there was still something missing.

Dad.

Desperate to feel some connection, I sneaked outside, closed my eyes and tried to imagine he was there, that we were having a conversation. As I created the scene in my mind, we appeared as two men of around the same age – myself slightly older. But in my gut, I was still his 11-year-old son. As much as he was frozen in time for me, I guess I would always be for him as well.

I started to speak and was filled with the excitement and exuberance of a child as I told him about everything that had happened since he left. He listened and smiled as I told him about my family and my career. When I talked about things I knew he wouldn't be pleased about, like drink and drugs, he let them slide because he knew that I was still learning. He seemed happy as we talked but I wanted to feel more. I wanted him to be proud of me. *Really* proud.

'I wrote a book, Dad. I told our story and I'm helping young people in the care sector. Kids like us. I'm trying to make a change,' I blurted out.

I waited for his reply but it never came.

Before I had a chance to go into more detail, to reel off my successes and plans, I heard a distant voice calling my name, dancing along the airwaves until it reached me and popped the bubble of my thoughts. It was Androulla.

'Are you going to come in?' she said, walking over and putting an arm around my shoulders. 'Everyone is asking for you.'

'In a minute,' I replied, clasping my hand over hers.

Deep down, I knew Dad would be proud. The problem was that I wasn't sure if I was proud of myself. I'd vowed to do something to help care kids – kids like him and me – and had helped some. But there was still a mountain to be climbed and, as I aged beyond him each year, it just felt like I was running out of time.

I started 2020 restless and unemployed. The consultancy work was trickling in but it was still sporadic and I needed some steady income while I built up the business. I wasn't sure what I was looking for but I knew that I would know as soon as I saw it. I circulated my CV and searched – not for jobs in semi-independent provisions but in charities, leadership organisation and community interest companies (CICs). I kept my eyes and my options open.

Then, one day, there it was. The perfect opportunity.

'The Roundhouse needs a youth project manager,' my recruiter, Milan, said.

I'd known about the Roundhouse Theatre for years. It is a hub of inspiration where artists and emerging talent from diverse backgrounds create extraordinary work together. Its ethos is based entirely on the idea that creativity has the power to change lives. It gives young people the chance to engage with the arts through music, media and performance projects, providing a safe space where they can grow as individuals.

Where they can thrive, rather than just survive.

It was something secure, something completely different, yet still within the realms of my experience. The charity had all the facilities and equipment to steer the youth away from the streets but they did not have the right foundations for safeguarding support, the expertise to know how to work with young people and other organisations involved in their care to ensure their health, safety and wellbeing was being properly looked after.

Which was where I could come in. I would be able to use my experience from managing semi-independent care homes and embrace and share my creative passions with the young people too – writing, painting and acting. I didn't just want the role, I was *desperate* for it.

I prepared obsessively for the interview and when I met with the head of youth services, Tina Randeen, it felt like magic; we chatted excitedly and immediately started bouncing ideas off one another. With my zealousness and her passion for her role, it felt like we could do anything.

I got the job and it was just the start to the year that I needed. I'd spent months feeling like something big was on its way and I'd just assumed it would be bad. It always had been in the past. Maybe this time, the instability and uncertainty was something that I needed to plough through before things started to go right.

Working at the Roundhouse, I felt like I had found my calling. My safeguarding experience, putting processes and procedures in place to ensure the safety and security of the young people, was vital and implemented brilliantly by the charity. I wasn't involved in the day-to-day wellbeing of the kids anymore – the keywork sessions and placement paperwork – I was there to help them grow creatively, channel their experience through the arts and help them onto a better path. There were moments when a wave of sadness would wash over me, when I realised how an opportunity like this could have transformed Alex or Daniel's lives. It broke my heart that they'd not been given that chance. But I had to look forward.

So I did.

Watching the confidence and skills of the children I was working with develop and listening to their dreams and ambitions gave me the same sense of hope that speaking to Isabella had. And it wasn't just in work that I felt better, either. Life at home was great and I was able to start looking after my health again. Working in the semi-independent provisions and even with the housing charities, I'd put my own wellbeing on the backburner. The precarious and unsafe situations the young people I was working with were in had made me sick with worry; barely sleeping, I tossed, turned and wracked my brains for solutions.

I know that Androulla had been worried, because she'd take any opportunity to point out that I couldn't help anyone if I wasn't well myself. She thought that all that exhaustion might even make me more susceptible to this new disease that had been found thousands of miles away in China, if it ever arrived.

'Look at this,' she said, as the news rolled a video of officials in hazmat suits checking the temperatures of residents in an apartment block in the city of Wuhan. 'You'd be floored if you got the flu at the moment and this looks far worse.'

'It's over in China,' I said.

'So was SARS at first,' she said.

I thought about how much noise had been made about SARS but how it never really landed in the same way here. But I didn't say anything to Androulla. I knew this wasn't really about this virus. The point she was making was that I needed to look after myself better. It was one of my first priorities after

I got the position with the Roundhouse, although the job itself boosted my health almost immediately anyway.

Rather than constantly being at war in the office, fighting for better support for kids who needed it from a system that just wanted to let them rot, I was providing effective and valuable support. I could leave work knowing my job was done for the day; it had made a difference and I could really enjoy my time with my own family for the first time in ages. I also found time to improve my own fitness and mental health. I joined a men's training group called Strength&. I'd had counselling when I was spiralling in the past, but it had never really worked for me, I found more solace and healing in physical activity and being part of a community. In my teens I'd found it in the boxing gym and now, in my forties, I found it in a muddy park in Hertford.

Everything had fallen into place.

I should have felt 100 per cent on top of the world and – personally – I did.

But the world around me *still* felt like it was vibrating with tension.

The virus Androulla had used to prod me about my health had been given a name:

Covid-19.

It was a 'novel coronavirus', a new virus that came from the same family as SARS. In a matter of three months, it had swept across large regions of China and had even made its way into Europe. The scenes coming out of Italy in particular looked like something from the set of an old war film – hospital corridors filled with people dangerously ill from this new and infectious respiratory disease, bodies piling up in morgues.

It was so close, yet still seemed so far.

After all, the only cases I'd heard about in the UK were those identified in the ex-pats they'd flown out of Wuhan and quarantined in an isolation ward of a hospital near Liverpool. The armed convoy had been followed by the media from RAF Brize Norton to Arrowe Park Hospital in Wirral and splashed all over the dinnertime news. But our government still seemed unconcerned. As cities across Europe began to shut down, life in the UK carried on much as normal, even big sporting events went ahead as planned.

'Sing "Happy Birthday" twice as you wash your hands.'

For weeks, that was the sum total of advice on the virus, bar one or two changes to travel advice that didn't affect most of us. Then, in mid-March, everything changed. The UK death toll from Covid-19 hit 55 and more than 1,500 cases had been identified. Many who had it were seriously ill. I watched as the prime minister, Boris Johnson, gave a televised press conference advising against non-essential travel and contact with others. He also advised that people avoided visiting pubs, clubs . . .

And theatres.

What did this mean for the Roundhouse?

Yes, we were a social venue by definition but we were also a lifeline for the young people we supported, too. I searched for clear definitions of 'essential' and 'non-essential' activities in the government communications, trying to find something that would indicate that we'd be able to keep on delivering services to our young people. It was all so woolly and confusing but I just couldn't imagine that they'd be closing a vital youth service. I decided to stop doom-scrolling and wait to discuss it with my line manager when I was next in. I was sure we could come up with a plan to ensure the groups could continue safely.

But then, later that day, I got an email asking me to go to our head office the following morning.

The silence was disconcerting as I was directed to a third-floor meeting room. It turned out I wasn't the only one to be pulled in unexpectedly. The room was filled with people from all areas of the organisation, their faces ashen and a low murmur of concerned and confused conversation rumbled around the room.

Everyone was awkwardly spread out. As well as hand sanitiser and regular hand washing, the government had also started advising people to keep a metre or so distance from others when indoors; 'social distancing' was how they'd labelled it. But despite the space between us, I could still feel the atmosphere pressing down on me, oppressive and tense. Questions hung in the air like dark clouds heavy with rain and I perched at the back of the room and rubbed my chin, perplexed. *What the hell is going on?*

Suddenly there was movement at the front of the room. The organisation's CEO had stood up and was raising her arms to appeal for quiet.

'Thank you all for coming in today,' she said. 'We realise it was short notice.'

Then she took a deep breath.

'The Roundhouse has made a conscious decision to close its doors with immediate effect due to the emerging coronavirus crisis,' she said. 'Please can everyone pack up their belongings and collect a laptop from the fourth floor so you are able to continue to work from home.'

My stomach lurched. *Do they mean me as well?*

The only thing I used my laptop for in work was to check and send emails. My job was physical, in-person, face-to-face with the young people. Surely they couldn't be sending me home to work? It was impossible.

As the news settled across the room, Tina called our team into another meeting room to explain the circumstances in more detail.

'With this virus circulating, we can't risk bringing people together until we know more. Until it's under control,' she said calmly.

'But what about the young people?' I asked.

'We're going to find ways to keep in contact,' she said. 'But we're going to have to take it one day at a time.'

I admired Tina's approach and I trusted her too.

No one had any answers. We had no idea what to do. But she was calm, collected and exceptionally good at moderating. Under her leadership, no problem felt too big to solve. If this was what the Roundhouse felt we needed to do, we'd make

238

it work between all of us. It wouldn't be for long, after all. Would it?

I collected my laptop as advised, left the building and decided to take a walk through Camden to clear my head and try to absorb what was happening. Of all the things I'd imagined, this wasn't one of them. But as I wound through the streets, I noticed other workers streaming out of office buildings, carrying bags and clutching laptops. Shops were pulling down their shutters and market stalls were being hastily packed up. I stopped and frowned. I'd assumed this was just a precaution that the Roundhouse was taking. The prime minister had advised people to avoid social venues like theatres so there was no point in staying open.

But shops and offices?

My phone vibrated with a BBC News alert, snapping me out of my thoughts: *Boris Johnson urges everyone to work from home if they can.*

I scanned the article, which said that the prime minister would address the nation later that day. I shook my head in disbelief.

Address the nation?

Not a news conference or a statement. He was going to *address the nation.* Every moment that passed, whatever was happening began to feel bigger. I looked up and continued watching office workers heading towards the tube. If it had been 5pm, it would have been like any other day. But it had only just turned noon. Even more bizarrely, people were stopping strangers in the street to ask what was going on. Back in Halifax, I wouldn't have batted an eyelid. But in London? That never happened.

I started to get a clearer sense of what was unfolding. I hadn't seen urgency and confusion like this since the 9/11 terrorist attack on the Twin Towers. Back then, I'd been working as a CHAPS payment inputter at the Halifax Building Society in my hometown. Everyone was glued to public TV screens and talking to strangers like they were old friends that day, united in horror.

The mood felt similar but this time the danger wasn't clear or present. It was creeping.

I looked up and noticed a dark cloud was blocking the cool March sun, high in the turquoise blue sky. Was this the big storm I'd felt coming? It was as if I'd stepped into a scene from an apocalypse movie where we weren't yet sure who or *what* the enemy was.

Instinctively, I dialled Androulla.

'They've sent us all home,' I said. 'It's crazy. I don't know what to do.'

'Just come home,' she said, her voice sweet and calm. 'We'll figure it out together.'

Later that evening, like the rest of the country, we sat together on the sofa and watched the prime minister's pre-recorded announcement. He spoke about the coronavirus and described it as an 'invisible killer'. He talked about how the virus was spreading rapidly and risked putting so pressure on the NHS that it would not be able to cope with the influx of patients.

Then he paused and looked directly into the camera: 'From this evening I must give the British people a very simple instruction – you must stay at home.'

I froze, open-mouthed and in shock at the enormity of the moment. This wasn't just the Roundhouse, or Camden, or London. This was the whole nation.

Going into a complete lockdown.

'We'll turn the tide in 12 weeks,' Boris had promised.

But I wasn't so sure.

As the news settled, a thousand thoughts whirled through my mind. But there was just one that my attention kept landing on.

What about the kids?

In the weeks that followed, more lockdowns and curfews were imposed across the globe. Overnight, we seemed to develop a whole new vocabulary around the virus – transmission, reproduction rate, viral load, self-isolation and mortality rate. The days were filled with fear and dread as daily government briefings charted the upwards trajectory of deaths from Covid-19.

The human impact of the government's hesitation to take serious action became rapidly apparent. As our death toll rose above 1,000, I could barely comprehend the statement from NHS England's medical director, Stephen Powis, that keeping the UK's death toll under 20,000 would be a 'good result'. The economy was at a standstill too, with businesses large and small struggling to survive, even despite support measures put in place. The charity sector was already on its knees after years of funding cuts as a result of the Conservative government's austerity measures, so I knew what was coming.

Four weeks after lockdown was announced, Tina called me.

'I'm so sorry, we're already struggling. We're going to have to let you go,' she said.

'Don't worry, I understand,' I said.

The same fate befell a few others who had started around the same time as I had.

The job had been my dream but none of us had anticipated the pandemic. The charity had to do what was necessary to come out the other side. They'd need to be there for young people after this. I couldn't even think about my own mortgage and bills because as more and more people lost loved ones, as children missed out on their education and unemployment rose, I could already see other pandemics looming on the horizon.

Child poverty.

Child mental health.

Child recruitment into crime.

All things the care sector was supposed to be there to prevent. All the things it had failed to deliver on for years even without being in a lockdown situation.

What the hell was happening to kids in care or in precarious situations right now? Who was looking out for the young people who didn't have the luxury of a family? Those who were isolated in a bedsit and couldn't communicate with the outside world because they didn't have a computer or even Wi-Fi?

If their support workers weren't turning up to work, who was helping them access the benefits they needed to ensure they could eat? What about the ones with health anxiety issues who might be too scared to go out to buy food but too poor to order in?

I felt like I was in the eye of a storm that was tearing violently through the lives of others who just weren't equipped to deal with its impact. I couldn't help everyone, but I knew I could help in the area I knew best.

So, unemployed once again, I turned my attention to how the pandemic and lockdown were affecting young people in the care sector. They were already marginalised, the very bottom of the priority pile, and I knew that now, the level of care and attention from local government and private providers would have dipped even lower.

Just four weeks into lockdown, reports started to emerge from the Department of Education highlighting concerns for looked after children who were going missing, and staff numbers being reduced in local authorities. Social workers were even being told to have no contact with their caseloads. While some fought these orders, others happily complied. I had no issue with those doing so because they were clinically vulnerable to the virus or shielding. But the ones who just didn't give a shit . . . They were just abdicating their responsibility to the young people in their care, seeing it as an opportunity for a holiday. It made my blood boil – but nowhere near as much as what happened next.

Because we were in a state of national emergency, the government was able to enact powers that allowed it to push through legislation that might ordinarily take months to bring into law. They used it for all kinds of things, like bypassing strict tender processes to allow them to procure personal protective equipment (PPE) and ventilators and giving police the power to fine individuals for breaking lockdown rules.

But on 23 April 2020 it published a statutory instrument – a form of law that allows the provisions of an Act of Parliament to be brought into force or altered without Parliament having to pass a new Act – that made around 100 changes to 10 sets of regulations related to the care and protection of vulnerable children and young people. Sixty-five safeguards for children in care were removed or diluted overnight. They gave local authorities the power to opt out of their children's social care duties from 24 April 2020 until 25 September 2020, a date that could at any point be extended or revoked.

The changes affected everything. From social worker visits and six-monthly reviews to adoption and children's placements outside their home areas, everything was stopped without any professional or public consultation and with no time for parliamentary scrutiny or debate. Changes that would ultimately cut off the country's most vulnerable young people from the fraying threads of support the system offered were made law without asking anyone with any relevant experience what the impact might be – and if there was a better way to do it. What made it even worse was that – unlike other legal changes made because of Covid-19 – this particular legislation hadn't been drafted in response to the crisis. It was a set of changes that the Conservatives had tried and failed to push through four years earlier. Back then, they'd proposed it as a change to allow local authorities to opt out of children's social care duties for up to six years as a trial for removing those duties altogether.

They'd faced such strong opposition that they'd had to backtrack. But now, here they were, pushing it through under the guise of helping local authorities deal with the pandemic. Just like they were ditching tender processes to give jobs – and millions of pounds – to their mates.

Even in a global crisis, the rich and powerful were looking after their own interests. Fuck what happens to the poor and unfortunate.

I felt sick to my stomach as the news filtered out of my TV. This irrational and mercenary decision-making would put so many in danger. I knew that all those vulnerable children were now more at risk than ever.

I couldn't just sit back and do nothing.

Article 39, a charity that fights for the rights of children in institutional settings, launched a petition to scrap the statutory instrument SI445. A Statutory Instrument is a form of legislation that allows the provisions of an Act of Parliament to be brought into force or altered without Parliament having to pass a new Act, basically making it quicker and easier to bring a law into force, without the same level of scrutiny.

I was the fiftieth person to sign the petition. As well as supporting campaigns, I started volunteering as a frontline worker, offering my services independently. I spent my days putting food parcels together and set up an online support group on Twitter and Facebook for young people in the care sector. Their social workers might not be going out to them but I was determined to find a way. So I set up Zoom meetings with those who had access to a laptop so that I could give advice when and where I could.

As the calls and messages flooded in, mainly from young people aged 17–25 who were in supported care and scared, the main issues became apparent. Young people had been left in the lurch without any support. Lots of local authorities had diverted their phones to an automated message telling callers that no one was available due to Covid-19 and that they needed to go online to request a call back.

If that sounds reasonable, given the circumstances, then you're reading from a point of privilege. For the young people who came to me, it was impossible. One young person contacted me when he didn't get his benefits paid as promised. He'd called his social worker who didn't pick up and her office had told him to book a call back online. When I spoke to him, he didn't have money for his electricity meter and he was in a state of distress.

I do not have a fucking computer and my bedsit has no Wi-Fi. And to top it off, the fucking library is closed. Can you help me? he said.

I started to get more and more messages like this from scared and angry kids who were skint. Many of them could not afford to eat.

I appealed on social media for people to donate anything they could. Money, food, toiletries, hand sanitiser – whatever they could manage. The response was overwhelming and I was able to put together hundreds of care packages filled with food and cleaning products and distribute them to young people in need in my local area. I dropped bleach and hand sanitiser off to young people who were living in semi-independent accommodation who had been totally neglected by the private companies that managed their houses.

I could make sure they had necessities, I could provide advice and try my best to get them any specific help they needed. I could help protect them from Covid-19 and hunger. But I couldn't protect them from those who would exploit the situation.

You see, without supervision in their accommodations, without school or college providing one good meal and a safe place for vulnerable and at-risk children to go, there was nothing to stop criminal gangs and abusers from preying on their desperation. They were like vultures circling, and not just around kids in the care sector but vulnerable children everywhere, like those living in dangerous and abusive homes who needed a way out.

Suffering violence and abuse.

Being hungry.

Not having enough money to pay your bills.

All of these factors, exacerbated by the crisis, were going unmonitored because the system was once again failing these young people.

In the face of being trapped with an abuser, starving or ending up homeless, and in the absence of support from the authorities that were meant to provide it, turning to criminal gangs became the only option for many.

It was survival instinct kicking in.

I could see it happening before my eyes but the rest of the country seemed oblivious.

One day, I was contacted by a journalist from the *Independent*, who asked me to comment on some statistics that the Metropolitan Police had provided, which indicated that there had been a reduction in crime during lockdown, particularly those crimes involving children in county lines.

'I'm sorry but I disagree,' I said.

'Excuse me?' she said.

'I disagree. It doesn't correlate at all with what we're seeing in the care sector,' I explained. 'Right now, staff aren't turning up to care homes. Social worker numbers have been reduced. Some young people are not receiving their weekly financial support and they get no answer when they call the council. Money is a matter of life or death for these young people. They don't have savings or families who can help them. If they don't get paid, they don't eat.'

'But the data provided by the police shows crime is down,' she pushed.

'They aren't looking at what's going on in these houses,' I said. 'They're focused on compliance with Covid measures. The scale of the problem hasn't revealed itself yet. These kids are desperate. If someone is going to give them £200 to deliver some drugs, they're going to do it.'

'But because of the reduced footfall on the streets, reduced traffic on the roads and on public transport, there is less anonymity for the dealers, isn't there? There's a higher chance of them sticking out like a sore thumb.'

I sighed down the phone. She was just doing her job. But the police and local authorities were churning out nonsense to cover up just how messed up things were. I'd heard reports from my peers working in care homes that their young people were going missing and it was not being properly investigated because of the lack of police available.

With a nation of people confined to their homes, the isolation and boredom taking its toll on all of us, many turned to their vices. Alcohol sales went through the roof, something many national newspapers reported with prominent splashes. But the stories about county lines kids being forced to dress up as couriers and Deliveroo drivers so they could drop drugs off undetected? They were lucky to scrape into the front half of even the most liberal of titles.

Any dealers the police would recognise – doing the kind of things they'd notice in 'normal' times – weren't anywhere near the streets anymore. They didn't need to be, because now they had enough desperate, unsupervised and unsupported young people to do their dirty work for them. The pandemic had changed all the rules. The criminal economy didn't stop because of a deadly virus killing thousands of people – it thrived. Young people were still going out and killing each other but no one cared. Children were being groomed for sexual exploitation but it was not hot news; it didn't sell papers or get a million views online. But it was still happening.

I found myself breaking down in tears on a daily basis.

I did what I could to help those who reached out to me but I was haunted by what was going on behind closed doors, up and down the country. Feeling powerless, I turned to social media and made a point of raising my concern every day. These young people had no voice so I had to make sure their needs were heard. I wasn't alone. Hundreds of amazing people joined with me to challenge the way our government was treating children and young people in the care sector at a time when they most needed support. Hundreds of voices using their platforms to ask the same thing – just what would it take for our government to protect our most vulnerable young people?

CHAPTER THIRTEEN

Pregnant and Alone

Alyssa

THE PANDEMIC COMPLETELY LAID bare all of the flaws in the system. The ones that professionals like me and those who were 'supported' by the care system had seen for years. The ones we'd raised with our superiors, local authorities and the government. The sector was in crisis, young people were in crisis and drastic changes were needed.

And what did we get?

A Department for Education report detailing the level of support care leavers should receive from councils. It contained some good ideas but nothing those of us in the sector hadn't already been screaming for at the tops of our lungs for years. Aside from that, it was best practice guidance, proposed targets to aim for – *nothing* that bound the councils to follow the guidelines by law.

In a sector strangled by austerity and poisoned by the greed of private companies, it was barely worth the paper it was written on. And in October 2020, seven months into a pandemic, when thousands of young people had already been forced into deeper poverty, been recruited into criminal gangs or seen their mental health deteriorate to the point of crisis, it was too little, too late.

That commissioned work had probably cost tens of thousands of pounds to complete. How much better could that time and money have been invested? How much faster could we have delivered the help our young people needed? I seethed with rage as the Education Secretary, Gavin Williamson, launched the report.

'The government is determined to break down the barriers our most vulnerable children and young people face,' he said.[1]

Oh yeah? I thought. *So why remove all those safeguards during a pandemic?*

Why, at a time when the nature of those in care was already changing, at a time when global events were exacerbating mental and physical health issues in young people, did they choose to pull their safety nets, like contact with social workers and access to support and social programmes?

I hadn't stopped working and volunteering throughout the Covid-19 crisis and I was mentally and physically drained. In my consulting capacity, I'd been going into organisations that were working with young people in the system both as a troubleshooter, advising them how they could provide better quality support, and as a safe pair of hands to roll my sleeves up and do the day-to-day work when staffing issues arose. Working

---

[1] www.cypnow.co.uk/news/article/government-lays-out-plan-to-support-care-leavers

with a charity dedicated to supporting vulnerable young people in particular, I saw and heard of so much pain and suffering. There was the teenage care leaver living in independent accommodation whose mental health had deteriorated so much that he'd stopped cleaning his room or himself. His support workers hadn't been round because of Covid-19, so no one had noticed his steady decline. I had to pull on rubber gloves and go in there myself to sort it out. I read about an autistic care leaver in his twenties, living independently, who was pinged to self-isolate by test and trace. During his quarantine, his food ran out and he had to skip meals, his electricity got cut off and the stress of his situation caused him to experience an emotional and mental shutdown while cooking. During the episode, a fire started and he had to be rescued and treated for smoke inhalation.

There were young people trapped in abusive homes, being groomed for sexual exploitation or criminal gain, and many who were pushed to self-harm and suicide due to the desperation of their situation. We were all living through the same pandemic, it just seemed like those that had the power to help deemed the lives of these young people less valuable than others who were affected.

Business owners, the elderly and the clinically vulnerable – the help for those groups was abundant and rightly so. But why did these young people not deserve the same support? Were they not our future, despite their shaky starts in life?

* * *

The potential of young people in the system had never escaped me. But the true extent of that potential never hit as hard as when I met Alyssa.

The first time we met was in her supported accommodation in November 2020; she was two months pregnant and searching for suitable accommodation for when the baby arrived. As we sat, socially distanced, going through the process, she started to open up to me about her life and feelings.

'I cannot remember a time when I've ever been truly happy,' she said.

She was 21 years old but wise beyond her years in many ways. I'd never worked with anyone like her before. The houses I'd managed accommodated young men. I'd worked with girls in children's homes at the start of my career and my campaigning and workshopping activities meant that I'd met care-experienced women like Desire and Isabella. But very few of my cases had ever been young women at the care cliff. None of them had been pregnant. It was a new experience completely and even our first meeting opened my eyes to even more issues in the system.

Alyssa had been homeless since she was 16. She'd lived with her aunt for a bit but that didn't work out. So, at 17 years old, Alyssa found herself couch hopping at friends' houses until her local authority could find her somewhere to live. When she couldn't find a spare sofa, she spent two months sleeping in doorways. At first, I was puzzled. She wasn't short of mates and many of them lived with their families in safe and comfortable homes. If my own daughter came to me in ten years' time and told me her female friend was sleeping in doorways in London while she waited to find somewhere to live, Androulla and I would open our door immediately. So why didn't Alyssa's friends' parents do the same?

'The whole process of trying to get help was like talking to a brick wall,' she said. 'Local authorities are very good at delegating responsibility and that's why nothing gets done. You need a referral to get a referral. When you call to speak to someone you're directed to the website where you have to fill out another form that's then passed onto an assessment centre who then pass it onto the housing team who take three months to respond and tell you that you forgot to fill out part B of the form, which means you have to start the process all over again and all the time the clock is tick, tick, ticking away. They don't seem to hear it, but you do.'

She didn't pause for breath as she ran through the cycle, only inhaling her frustration when she was finished. I was exhausted just hearing what she'd gone through but I knew exactly what she meant. I'd seen paperwork circulate around council offices like a paper aeroplane that never reached its destination.

'How does that make you feel?' I asked.

'Well, the time doesn't stop. But your patience does. You start to lose the plot. Anyone would. I swear they do it so you'll give up,' she said, shaking her head. 'No one wants someone like me living in a decent flat in London.'

She was right. I'd seen it a thousand times. For landlords, a care leaver came with history. It didn't matter whether it was their fault or not. Rather than seeing the potential to give a young person a chance to make their way in life, they see the threat of future headache caused by unnecessary calls, rent arrears, complaints about living conditions. London properties, even poor-quality ones, could command big money without the complications of tenants living on universal credit and housing support.

'Couldn't you stay with friends when you found yourself homeless?' I asked, still confused as to why no one offered to help, even temporarily.

'My ex, he was trouble,' she said. 'My friends' parents didn't want that around them. He was still in my life then, so where I was, he'd always show up. I understood why they didn't need that.'

Alyssa's now ex-boyfriend was notorious in east London where she grew up. He had a reputation for being violent, especially towards women. But that didn't deter a teenage Alyssa.

'When we met, I was the best in my class at school,' she said. 'I got all my grades but when I left that's when it all went wrong. You see, I would have done anything for him at the time.'

And she did. She was young and smitten. So she didn't recognise when his love made way for obsession and control. He would demand she steal things from the high street, things he could sell, like perfume and baby clothes.

'What if you refused?' I asked.

'That's when he'd get violent. So I stopped saying no,' she said.

After that, Alyssa's relationship followed a well-worn path. I'd seen it myself when my own mother's violent ex gaslighted her, manipulated her, beat her and forced her to cut ties with her family. I knew how controlling men like Alyssa's ex could be. And I knew how clever they could be too.

'Did your mum see what he was doing to you?' I ventured, although I already knew the answer.

'Not at first,' she said. 'He was always kind and polite in front of her. He knew how to act up in front of people. That was his trick.'

'But when you were alone. . .' I began and Alyssa nodded.

'As soon as were on our own he would grab my neck and say nasty things to me,' she said.

'Like what?' I asked.

'He'd call me a fat cunt or a slut,' she said. 'He made me feel worthless.'

'Did you go to the police?' I asked.

'Of course,' she said. 'But nothing happened.'

'What about your mum?' I asked.

'I know she was worried. But she couldn't handle the pressure,' Alyssa said. 'She never knew where I was, if I was coming home. If I was even alive. I'm not surprised she kicked me out.'

Alyssa blamed herself for getting caught up in the wrong crowd but she was just too young to make good choices. Without her mum's guidance, professional support or anyone taking her cries for help seriously, what was she supposed to do?

Even when she tried, Alyssa could not shake her then-boyfriend off. She began to accept his catalogue of abuse as normal.

'Once he locked me in a cupboard for two days with no food or water. He wouldn't let me go to the toilet. I can't even remember what I did to deserve that. Maybe nothing,' she said. 'He'd bully anyone who made friends with me and if anyone tried to help me, he would accuse them of plotting against him.'

Thankfully for Alyssa, fate interjected. He was arrested for armed robbery and jailed for 15 years.

'I was finally able to move on with my life,' she said. 'After that, I decided that I would never let anyone control me like that again.'

Learning when her ex had been jailed and knowing when her baby was due, it was apparent that her ex was not the father but I waited for Alyssa to tell me as much.

'I did meet someone after that, obviously,' she said, pointing to her stomach. 'But that didn't work out. I was stronger this time. I decided it was over and I left.'

Alyssa made the decision to have the baby and bring it up as a single parent. She made no bones about the fact that it would be much better to have the extra support of a partner but she'd vowed never to live under the ominous cloud of a man again.

'Every day I would tell myself that I was in the driving seat. I was in control,' she said. 'Eventually I believed it and now that's the way I like it.'

Alyssa's supported accommodation was fine for just her but she knew she'd need to move as soon as the baby arrived. It was my job to help her find safe and suitable accommodation in time. When we started working together, she was embroiled in the bidding process for council properties and needed some guidance to make the right choices.

'How does it feel being pregnant, living in supported accommodation and getting ready to live on your own with a baby?' I said.

'Does it matter how I feel?' she shrugged. 'I have no choice.'

We sat together looking at the properties available to her in the London area. Most of the flats she was offered were box-sized and situated ten floors up in concrete tower blocks with no lift access. They were barely suitable for *anyone*, let alone a young single mum who'd have to drag a pushchair up and down each day. I don't know if it was the dark winter nights or the shadow of Covid, but I felt thoroughly useless. There was nothing I could do for her except tell her to keep declining the properties until she was offered something appropriate.

'Chris, they're saying if I keep turning them down there will be nothing left,' she said. 'They're saying we'll be homeless.'

Alyssa was always calm and collected but I could hear panic rising inside her. It was rising in me too. I didn't want her to end up with nothing but I couldn't allow her to accept the hovels she was being offered. I couldn't see a new life starting there but I could see the cycle starting again.

'Just hold out a bit longer,' I said, praying something better would come up.

Throughout the process, I noted the prejudice that Alyssa faced. We'd just experienced a summer of protests against systemic racism both in the UK and US. The Black Lives Matter movement had forced us all to challenge our bias and wake up to our privilege. Watching Alyssa – a black, 20-something mum-to-be – fight for the most basic human requirements for her and her baby, I noticed that most of the people making decisions on her behalf were white, middle-class women in their forties and fifties. What did they know of her struggle? Her needs?

What did I know?

There is already a stigma attached to young, single, pregnant girls. Add race into the mix and that stigma is multiplied. Alyssa had already told me that she'd been frowned upon by authorities who knew nothing about her circumstances.

'They see me as garbage, Chris,' she said. 'They think I'm just another problem looking for an easy ride.'

It couldn't have been further from the truth. Alyssa had redeemed any wrongdoing in her life. She worked two jobs, as a cleaner and in online sales. I told her I was worried about her because I'd seen lots of kids from care settings get roped into online selling scams. No sale, no pay. But Alyssa assured me she was fine.

'It gives me a little extra cash,' she said. 'Not much but it all helps.'

She spent any spare time she had reading and studying. She was determined to get an education and then a career.

'It's not just for me. Or for my baby,' she said. 'It's for all those other young girls who will follow in my footprints.'

After six weeks of declining properties, a shared house with another young girl became available. In all honesty, it wasn't ideal. It wasn't what I'd want for my daughter and it wasn't what I wanted for Alyssa. But time was running out and it was the only clean and safe place available.

'It is what it is,' Alyssa said, with a knowing smile.

I was disappointed for her. I was angry at the system for not providing better support for Alyssa and a better start for her baby. But I knew that Alyssa was strong, both physically and mentally. She was more than capable of taking good care of herself and her baby.

By the time her son was born in May 2021, the world was changing and Alyssa was moving with it. She had decided life would be different for him. Her boy would not fall victim to the failings of the state, as she did. He would have a life full of love. She would work every hour God sent to make sure he always had food on the table, new clothes on his back. Even when she was exhausted from her double shifts, she would make time to read and play. Each night she would kiss him and vow to always protect him always. There would be no second best for her boy. He was going to grow into adulthood prepared with all the right tools. He'd be kind and courteous to women always. She'd make sure he stuck with education, even when he rebelled against it, because that was how he would build his future. That was how he would access the same opportunities as his peers from other backgrounds.

Alyssa had suffered her whole life but she wasn't using her experience to get an easy ride, like the stereotypes suggest. She was utilising her past to pave the way for her baby boy. Where she had to crawl, he would glide. There would be no barrier to his dreams and the colour of his skin would blend into the society like a rainbow.

Where she had survived, he would thrive.

The hand that rocks the cradle is the hand that rules the world.

The cycle of destruction can stop with Alyssa and other young mums just like her. If only the system would allow it.

Around the time I met Alyssa, I also found out that I was going to be a dad again. I think that's why in part her situation and story had such a profound impact on me. I was shocked at first because Androulla and I had tried for many years to have another baby after Antonia but it just never happened. We'd both accepted it and nestled into the family unit we'd made.

The news was one of the magical things to come out of the second national lockdown for us. A crack of light in the darkness. Of course, around the same time another wave of Covid-19 was crashing across the country with cases and deaths rising anew. Separated from friends and family, it was a hard time for anyone to be going through a pregnancy.

But a young, first-time mum going through it alone?

It didn't even bear thinking about.

The fact that Alyssa's pregnancy pushed her higher up the bidding queue for council housing would be a bone of contention for some. There is this idea that young girls are going out and getting themselves pregnant just to bump them up the list. That kids from care backgrounds in particular have an almost Machiavellian understanding of the system and how they can exploit it. But broadly speaking, that's not how it works.

In fact, I'd argue any care leavers using pregnancy to try to get better housing don't know the system as well as they think because it's certainly not a guarantee. There are thousands of young people waiting for suitable accommodation and a finite supply of houses. These houses are allocated using a ridiculous process.

First of all, you have to be nominated and that all depends on how well you are doing. If a young person has a good track record of paying bills and they're in education or employment, then they get to the top of the housing queue quicker than most. What this means is the system is automatically biased. It prefers those who are working and older. That's why we have so many homeless teenagers and young adults. They haven't had the support or guidance they desperately needed.

So they fall through the cracks.

Then there's a ridiculous points system. To be able to bid for a house, you need a certain number of points. But you can't pick *where* you want to live. Care leavers are only allowed to bid for properties in certain areas – mostly deprived and crime-ridden. And let's not forget that of that finite supply of houses, a significant proportion aren't fit for a dog, let alone a human being.

The system segregates young people in the care sector from their peers. The law is different for young people who live at home with Mum and Dad and those aged 16–18 who are in care. There's no legal protection, leaving them high and dry and putting them at risk. And who is more vulnerable than a young, single, first-time mum, learning to live alone for the first time in the middle of a global pandemic?

I am not underestimating the strength and capability of these young women. To the contrary, I believe they have more power to make change than most of us. The actress Samantha Morton is a prime example. She grew up in the foster system and suffered sexual abuse. She left the care sector as a young mum and used her experiences as a catalyst to succeed and act as a voice for other care leavers.

But not all will thrive regardless of what life throws at them. Some of them need a little more help.

The Department for Education report outlines guidelines for the support that care leavers who are pregnant or who have children should receive but it doesn't go far enough. It doesn't challenge the stigma they face; it certainly doesn't tackle the racism that Alyssa faced and it doesn't even acknowledge the impact of the pandemic. In fact, the government didn't even include care leavers and the organisations that support them in coronavirus bailout plans.

Call me cynical, but it's as if they want these kids to fail.

The world is tough for every care leaver but for those who leave with a baby it's even more difficult. They have to work even harder because another life depends on their survival. Despite all their efforts, our broken system too often fails them.

It's a point where the cycle can end or start again.

Too often, the system perpetuates the latter.

CHAPTER FOURTEEN
Restoration

YOU KNOW THE OLD nursery rhyme 'The House that Jack Built'? The cumulative tale of how Jack's shoddy work building a house eventually went on to have a much wider impact? My dad used to quote it all the time when I was growing up in Boothtown in Halifax. We lived in a draughty old house and things always needed fixing but I don't really remember it as being in a state of disrepair.

Maybe that's because my dad was forever hammering something to the wall, filling holes in here and there and patching up the cracks as they appeared. When it rained – which was pretty often in West Yorkshire – water would come flooding in through gaps that routinely appeared in the window frames. Mum would be rushing around with towels to stop the rain getting onto the carpet but she'd be smiling as she did it.

My parents were incredibly good at making everything seem OK, even when they weren't. That's just what they did. It was what lots of parents did. They considered their only important job to be keeping me and my sister Donna safe and making sure we did not stress about unnecessary things. Dad often did this by turning challenging situations into a game.

'Quick, put your raincoats on and start building a boat,' he'd say as droplets started falling from the aging roof as well. 'There's not much time.'

We'd squeal with excitement and put on our wellies and waterproofs as Mum produced the plastic shopping bags that she saved in abundance from the kitchen cupboards. We'd rummage around for empty pop bottles and use sticky tape to fashion a bodged boat that we'd be able to set sail in, should the perilous waters rise too high. While we laughed and created, we were distracted, allowing our parents to tackle the problem without placing even an ounce of the burden of worry on us.

As a parent myself now and a professional supporting hundreds of young people, I believe that's one of your most important tasks. Don't let your children see you suffering. Don't expose them to problems that should not yet be their concern. As a child, I never really noticed how patched together our house was. Truth be told, I think I only *really* got it when I bought my own house 25 years later and was faced with the challenge of fixing the constant niggles and issues on a restricted budget.

'They must have built this house on a Friday,' I'd say to Androulla when the boiler broke or the pipes froze in winter. It was another of my dad's favourite sayings.

'What do you mean?' she asked, the first time I said it.

I'd laughed, realising that despite losing him so young, I still had some of my old man in me.

'It means it must have been built on a Friday because it's falling to pieces. The builders will have rushed to finish so they could get to the pub.'

As an adult, I'm convinced the house that Jack built was constructed on a Friday. I'm also fairly certain that the current care system was thrown together in haste at the end of the week too. In fact, I've come to use 'The House that Jack Built' as a way to describe the care sector for young people, highlighting how every individual failing connects to another, leaving a creaking structure that no old plastic bags and pop bottles could patch up.

In many ways, that's what we've been doing for years now – campaigners, charities and those frontline staff working with young people day in and day out who are committed to their obligations and often go over and above. When the water pours in, we've been patching things up the best we can. As it's become too much to stop the water getting in, we've put on our coats and wellies, grabbed those empty pop bottles and bags and tried to build a makeshift boat big enough to fit and support all of the young people entering care in the UK.

But those numbers are increasing.

Our resources are running out, due to the impact of austerity.

Now we're just bailing out to keep the damn boat afloat.

We can't continue like this.

In December 2020, the latest annual Department for Education statistics on children in care and care leavers was released. The number of children in care had increased by 2 per cent from 2019 to 80,080.[1] But looking at figures since 2009, that number had increased by 31 per cent. Some were quick to point out that the rate of growth had slowed slightly but, working in the sector, I know that this barely provides an inch of breathing space in a system that is already at crisis point.

Growth might have slowed, but it's still consistent and continuous. There is no let up.

Analysis of the report by the policy and participation manager of the charity Become 1992, Sam Turner, which was condensed into a widely shared Twitter thread,[2] also identified a swathe of regional differences. He highlighted that between 2015 and 2020, the number of children in care in London had increased by 0.4 per cent, while in the North East the increase was 34 per cent.

When it came to looking at *who* was in care, there were significant differences; for example, 30 per cent of people in care in London are Black or Black British, whereas in the North East, this figure was just 2 per cent. In terms of ages, 37 per cent of those in care in London were aged 16–17 and dangerously close to the 'care cliff', while in the North East this figure was

---

[1] explore-education-statistics.service.gov.uk/find-statistics/children-looked-after-in-england-including-adoptions/2020

[2] twitter.com/samtrner/status/1337033869887934465

16 per cent, with half of all children in care being under ten years old.

These differences are vital when considering how we might improve the care system across the nation. I couldn't have said it better myself than Sam Turner when he said: 'There is not one care system.'

Our most vulnerable young people are not one homogeneous mass, but individuals with different experiences, needs and hopes. Yet they have been othered without any consideration of these for far too long. Care kids vs 'normal' kids. This has to stop.

It was hard to feel any sense of hope as 2020 drew to a close and 2021 dawned. Many in the sector found ourselves cut off from young people in our care, struggling to find inventive ways to maintain something that looked like support at a time when we knew they needed it most. I had a clear intention. I wanted to make waves. Stir up a storm and get the backing of the care community across social media platforms. I wanted us to use the pandemic as an opportunity to restore the care sector, to start building from the foundations again. I wanted to put young people in care – REAL young people who are in care NOW – at the forefront of everyone's mind. Not the stereotyped ne'er do well. Not the sanitised and hand-picked for a government panel version.

The Taylors, Yonahs and Daniels. The Ifazes, Dardans and Isabellas, the Alexes and Alyssas.

The truth of the sector. Rather than what the government wants you to see.

I had witnessed it first-hand going through the system myself. While working in children's homes and while working with young people aged 16-plus in the sector. I had seen the mass negligence in public settings and private sector. Through my work with the *Newsnight* team, I'd seen the true spread of the issue across the country. Even reading the papers, I saw examples of failures every single day.

There was the care worker who had specialised in working with gang-affiliated youths and then turned her hand to county lines, after starting a relationship with one of the boys she supported. Together, they used her access to vulnerable people to recruit mules. When the police finally caught her, the two boys she was found with had 191 wraps of heroin inside them. A death sentence if they'd burst.[3]

There was the young mum who hadn't been properly supported after leaving a mother and baby unit, who plunged to her death from her entirely inappropriate accommodation in the upper floors of a high-rise flat in Enfield.[4]

There was the revelation that child refugees had been illegally detained in the UK between April and September 2020 after crossing the Channel to escape poverty and persecution. One was even held for around 65 hours – 41 hours over the legal

---

[3] www.bbc.co.uk/news/uk-england-devon-55561327

[4] www.mirror.co.uk/news/uk-news/enfield-murder-first-picture-mum-14267240 and www.dailymail.co.uk/news/article-7824157/Police-warn-gang-murder-investigations-blocked-wall-silence.html

limit and without proper sleeping facilities or access to fresh air.[5] It was disgusting, disheartening and devastating.

No matter how loud I screamed, no matter how many more joined in, the message that kept bouncing back to me from inside the walls of government was always the same:

If it's not broken, why fix it?

I began to wonder if they were looking at the same system as I was. A system so damaged that everything attached to it was ceasing to work as well, all the parts spinning out and destroying lives as they went. Then I realised. Why would those in power want to acknowledge a system that they'd built – like Jack and on a Friday – then destroyed through years of austerity?

This is the system our government built
    This is the underfunded council that's been crushed by the system the government built
    This is the private landlord that feeds off the desperation
    That was caused by the system our government built

As I considered the state of the system, I couldn't help thinking about Mum and Dad and how, despite our house's creaking foundations and cracked windows, despite being short on money and weighed down by stresses, they always found a way. They fulfilled their role as parents.

---

[5] www.independent.co.uk/news/uk/home-news/children-refugees-channel-detained-home-office-b1798100.html

Why is the state as a corporate parent not able – *or not willing* – to do the same?

When I left my role as home manager in 2017, I started interviewing at various companies that provided accommodation for young people aged between 16 and 21. Many of the properties I visited were not suitable for wild animals, never mind vulnerable kids. One house was covered in damp and my shoes stuck to the carpet as I followed the private landlord across the living room.

'Just put a nice picture of a rainbow in the hallway,' he said. 'It will look better.'

I was shown round another by a young employee who I doubted had the experience to support the young people, which was why I was being invited in. As I'd approached the house, I'd noticed a broken window and pointed it out to her.

'Yeah, that's Gemma's bedroom. It's been like that for a few weeks now,' she shrugged. 'Every time we get it fixed she just breaks it, so we've left it to teach her a lesson.'

Another house, home to six young people aged between 16 and 19, had a leaky roof and was infested with mice that were nibbling through electrical cables and shitting all over the place. Its residents didn't even bat an eyelid. They seemed unaffected by the putrid smell and had learned to dodge the growing droplets of water cascading onto them. It was as if they'd accepted that was all they deserved.

Think about that for a moment.

Then imagine this. A kid – maybe even *your* kid – a child from a 'normal' home and 'normal' background, lying in a hospital bed in a damp room, with water dripping through the roof and mice scurrying around them. The media would have a field day. There would be outrage and consequences. Staff would be struck off. Wards would be closed. Rightly so, because they'd failed in their duty of care.

Correct?

Yet the equivalent happens every second of every day in the care sector and no one says a word.

In three years since those visits, nothing has changed. Even in January 2020, I visited a group of houses that were in a similar state of disrepair. Despite all the noise and all the voices speaking out for kids in the care sector, the investigations and statistics that back up the issues they are raising, nothing is being done and the system is nowhere near fit for purpose. And this is even before we fully understand the impact that the pandemic has had on the care sector.

The state is failing in its duty as corporate parents, pleading poverty when the private landlords it has outsourced its responsibility to are stacking up the cash that comes in every week from local authorities, never spending a penny on the young people it is intended to support.

Care workers like myself struggle to squeeze even the most basic necessities out of those who hold the purse strings, let alone any little luxuries to make life more bearable for kids who have already suffered so much. And as for support for complex needs, forget it. I'm not a trained therapist but I've had to take on the role of counsellor because the young people in my care could not get the therapeutic support they needed from the authorities. You start your career as a care worker but as the cracks appear, you realise you have to be so much more than that. We are teachers, counsellors, painters and decorators, plumbers, electricians. Honestly, a lot of the time I doubt we're working within what we're legally allowed to but what choice do we have?

If you care, you care, and that's what keeps this broken system hanging on by a thread.

But I'm not sure that's going to be enough for much longer.

The one glimmer of hope for anyone who gives a damn has been the care review that the Conservative government promised in its 2019 election manifesto. It was a commitment to look at the care system to make sure that children and young adults get the support they need from the state.

Eagerly anticipated, there were still concerns.

Who would be appointed to oversee the review?

Would the voices of care-experienced people and those presently in care be represented?

Would it look at the care sector as a whole and not just stop at 18?

In November 2020, as the wheels for the review began to be set in motion, I wrote to the children's commissioner for England, Anne Longfield, to voice my personal concerns, ones that I knew were reflected by professionals across the sector.

It was the continuation of a discussion that I'd had directly with Anne, while I'd been campaigning.

'We have spoken previously about the lack of experience within central government when it comes to politicians and ministers who lack any first-hand experience of the care sector, lived or professional,' I said. 'How can the review be taken seriously if we have no one to represent the care sector?'

I went on to raise my ongoing concern about the vast outsourcing of support provisions to the private sector and the impact this was having on young people up and down the country.

'I was recently asked in an interview to explain the difference between what the private and the public elements of the care sector provide. Back in the 1990s, private settings did not really exist. Yet now they dominate the whole care sector. The best explanation I could give, based on my lived and professional experience, is this: the public sector offers care professionals and young people a safety net that they will at some point need. The private sector offers no safety net whatsoever. So if you fall, you fall.'

I listed again the mass failings I'd personally witnessed, from profit being put before people to kids being recruited into county lines and watching young care leavers fall off the care cliff into homelessness. I asked for the whole picture to be considered in the review and implored that an independent regulator be established, focused solely on children and young people in care.

It is no exaggeration that the care review represents a once-in-a-generation chance to effect real change. To start again and give children and young people in care the support they need.

The support they deserve.

It's a chance to truly 'build back better', to borrow an over-used phrase from the growing pandemic buzzword bingo book. We are at a tipping point and what happens next will ripple through generations to come. I'm trying to be positive but it's hard when the government seems to have tripped at the first hurdle.

On 15 January 2021, Education Secretary Gavin Williamson formally launched the care review with a speech that acknowledged some of the current system's failing. He said: 'We have known for some time that despite the best efforts of hardworking and dedicated social workers, the children's social care system is not delivering a better quality of life and improved outcomes for those it is designed to help. This review will be bold, wide-ranging and will not shy away from exposing problems where they exist.'[6]

Then, he announced the individual who would oversee the review – Josh MacAlister, a social entrepreneur and former teacher.

A former social worker or care professional?

No.

Care-experienced?

---

[6] www.theguardian.com/society/2021/jan/15/childrens-social-care-to-undergo-major-overhaul-in-england

No.

The chief executive of Frontline, an organisation that seeks to fast-track graduates into social work?

Yes.

An organisation that was launched in 2013 with the help of a £1-million government start-up grant approved by the then-education secretary Michael Gove?

Yes.

An organisation that is chaired by Camilla Cavendish, a former head of the No. 10 policy unit under David Cameron?

Yes.

MacAlister *is* stepping down from Frontline to lead the review but I can't deny that his ties to the government are a cause for concern. Carolyne Willow, the director of Article 39, a charity that fights for the rights of children in care, said it 'sounds like the government already knows what it wants to happen next in children's social care'. It's unsurprising that many care-experienced people feel the same.

Can this review really be independent?

There have been some steps in the right direction, though. Since the launch of the care review, an 'Experts by Experience' advisory panel – a small group of hand-selected individuals with experience of the children's social care system – has been appointed, and I am one of its members.[7] I have also been invited

---

[7] www.cypnow.co.uk/news/article/care-review-officially-launches-as-experts-panel-revealed

to join the care review's design panel, which will work on creating a new model for the system. There are early positive signs, but I am still cynical. What comes out of the review is a report. A series of recommendations. But what then? How will we be able to push for those changes?

Despite all my misgivings, though, I am fighting to stay positive. I hope that I can use my experience and my knowledge to drive change. And I hope that MacAlister stays true to his commitment at the launch review, the promise that he will 'deliver a wide-ranging plan to extend the joy, growth and safety of childhood and the esteem, love and security of family life to all children'.

ALL children.

I hope that he will step up to the challenge because it's the only chance we have to make real change. What comes next has to be revolutionary.

It has to be radical.

It has to rip up all the rule books, tear up the corporate contracts.

It has to REALLY start again.

Anything less won't be good enough for our kids and our once-in-a-generation opportunity will be squandered.

CONCLUSION

The Power of Dreams

SO, AS WE STAND on this precipice – this tipping point for a sector upon which tens of thousands of vulnerable young people depend – what is the answer? What can be done to transform the lives of children and young people in care in the UK, now and in the future?

From a professional standpoint, I believe corporate corruption is the rot spreading through the already rickety foundations of the system. It needs to be expunged immediately. The private sector and its greedy landlords have been allowed to run riot for too long, sucking everyone around them into their money-driven orbit, making even the most committed care worker compliant by association. They have profited off the most broken and damaged children for long enough and they now should not only be stopped but held to account too.

If there is to be accountability, there needs to be regulation. And not just Ofsted extending into the area of post-16 support – not when its approach is already strangling children's homes in red tape. The children's care sector needs a dedicated and independent regulator to apply all the checks and balances necessary to keep our vulnerable young people safe, sector employees supported and the system *working*.

The state should afford young people in care the same status as their peers who are not in the system. A child – *any* child – should be considered a child until they are 18. A tough upbringing and trauma should not see a child in care at the age of 16 or 17 treated any differently. They should not have to pull themselves up by their bootstraps because of where circumstances out of their control have led them. If anything, if a child has suffered abuse, trauma or neglect then we should be giving them *more* support than a child from a 'normal' background – not less.

Nor should there be segregation within the sector itself. The lives of unaccompanied asylum-seeking children are no less valuable or important than the lives of at risk children from the UK. A child in care – no matter where they are from or their circumstances – is still a child.

Full stop. No ifs or buts about it.

Those in their ivory towers – the politicians and policymakers – should look at the provisions available to young people in the care sector and think 'that would be good enough for my child' rather than recoiling in horror and thinking 'my baby doesn't deserve that'.

Neither do the kids in care.

A child or young person in care is no less equal than one who is not. If you see your 24-year-old son or daughter as a young person that still needs support as they develop and grow, occasional guidance to navigate mistakes and challenges, then why is it any different when that 24-year-old is a young, single mum, who grew up in care home because her parents were drug addicts?

More than anything, those in power need to stop looking away when these young people turn 18. The care cliff needs to end. Rather than turning their backs while child after child plummets off the edge, with no safety net and no hope, a sturdy bridge into adulthood needs to be provided. No child should ever, ever be forced to leave care if they are not prepared to do so.

But what I want, and what other care-experienced professionals and organisations that lobby for the rights of care kids want, is not what matters the most. What matters the most is what children in care, care leavers and care-experienced young people want and need. They too have needs and wants. They have dreams and they should be heard.

For this to ever work, they *must* be heard.

From my time both living and working in the care sector, I have realised that every young person wants to believe in magic – even if they'd never admit it. It comes from a place of wanting to be accepted, of wanting to be heard and wanting to be the master of their own destiny. It comes from a place of feeling that some supernatural intervention is the only way you will ever get on in life.

Magic gives wings to dreams.

But today, young people in the care system are plagued by their dreams because they feel impossible and out of reach.

Outside of the care sector, talk of adolescent dreams conjures up grand and outlandish wishes. Fanciful fun. Fame, fortune and a 100 million followers on Instagram. A Ferrari and a mansion in Beverly Hills. But the dreams that seem out of reach to children in care bear no resemblance.

I want a safe place to live.

I want a family.

I want someone to love me.

Material trappings have little meaning for them. Being able to wake up in the morning and feel safe, wanted and accepted is far more valuable. How have we reached a point where it has come to this? How have the things most of us take for granted become so unreachable to these children that it tortures them?

In Lemn Sissay's view, kids in care are superheroes and in a dream world they'd be treated as such. Their unconventional routes into the world would make them like an Umbrella Academy of sorts. Under the watchful eye of committed professionals, they would be provided with the tools to find and make the most of the exceptional skills that lay hidden beneath. They would be supported through their trauma and be taught how to heal. No child in the academy would be viewed as more important than the rest; no child would be allowed to fall behind and no child would be asked to leave until they were prepared to face the world alone. And then, when they were ready – *only* when they were ready – the doors of the academy would be flung open and they'd be able to soar seamlessly into their futures, their past a superpower rather than a burden.

Take this out of the fantastical setting and tell me, what's so hard about delivering just that?

Rather than leaving them to rely on magic, our care system needs to be the thing that gives flight to their dreams. Supported by passionate key workers who are focused on ensuring every young person succeeds in the independent world, they should be walking into jobs, paying rent on nice apartments and starting businesses, families and movements that will change the world.

They're not asking for it to be easy. They're just asking for it to be an option. For exactly the same chance as other kids.

There should be no need for magic, just parity and fairness.

It is 30 years since my own journey in the care system began. Three whole decades since my dad passed away. Looking back at my own life, I have no regrets about the things I did, or how my life turned out. Of course I wish my dad hadn't died and I prefer not to have been mixed up in criminal activity and drugs as a teenager. But it happened and I got through it.

Every day I tell my story to the young people I work with in the hope that they can take something positive from it. Nobody wants to be brought up through the care system but many will be. In the aftermath of the pandemic, with rising poverty and the increased prevalence of mental health issues and crises, the numbers are more likely to grow than reduce. We cannot stop people ending up in the system but we can create a better system for them to be in.

When I think about the system and all its flaws, my mind is constantly taken back to *Oliver Twist*. It might look different but the fundamentals that underpin the fictional Mudfog workhouse are still present in the system today. Segregation and othering. Desperation and an internal and external belief that its inhabitant's futures are pre-determined. What comes next cannot be a model built on Victorian England.

It cannot be the system that traumatised my dad.

It cannot be the system that scarred me and extinguished the potential of so many.

It cannot be the system we have now.

It has to be something new, something better and informed by those who now rely on it.

We need to remove the stigma and rewrite the 'care kid' story that has been retold for generations. We need to understand their dreams, their potential and create safe paths for them to follow.

When they ask, 'Please, sir, can I have some more?' there should only be one response.

'Yes, you can.'

Useful Resources

Become
www.becomecharity.org.uk
Charity providing help and advice for children in care and young care leavers.

Street Angels
www.streetangels.org.uk
Network of Christian volunteers helping homeless people and others in need.

Article 39
article39.org.uk
Charity fighting for the rights of children in institutional settings.

Christian Action Housing Association
www.christianaction.org.uk
Social landlord that provides accommodation in four north London boroughs.

Care Review website

www.gov.uk/government/groups/independent-review-of-childrens-social-care

Government website about the independent review of children's social care.

Hub of Hope

hubofhope.co.uk

The Hub of Hope is a mental health support database created by Chasing the Stigma.

You can download the free app, visit the website, or text HOPE to 85258 to find help.

Samaritans

www.samaritans.org

116 123

jo@samaritans.org

Samaritans operates a 24-hour service available every day of the year.

PAPYRUS

www.papyrus-uk.org

0800 068 41 41

PAPYRUS supports teenagers and young adults who are feeling suicidal.

RT Group

www.rt-group.co.uk

Trusted recruitment and consultancy partners for local authorities across the UK, specialising in Social Care, Education and Occupational Health.

Acknowledgements

TOWARDS THE END OF 2018, I was sitting back in my armchair looking at the bookshelf and thinking maybe it's time to write another book. *Damaged* opened so many doors for me and I didn't want them to close. As I'd continued in my career I realised I needed to carry on because there was so much more to write about.

This would never have happened without the amazing team at Blink Publishing. Beth Eynon, I am forever indebted to you. From day one you have always believed in me and my work. You have vision beyond words.

Nikki Girvan, my writing partner. You are the Carol Vorderman of words. Thank you for your honesty and talent. Without you, my books wouldn't exist.

Karen Stretch and Ali Nazari, thank you for looking after the publication side of things. The A Team.

Brett Sizeland, Scott Wilkinson and the whole team at Strength&. My world has really changed, both physically and mentally, since joining the group and my life has flourished. Thank you for pushing me hard and making me believe in myself again. Will, Big Dog, all you guys.

Thank you to Paul Owen and the team at Caring Hearts Fostering. Paul, you have been my go-to man throughout. Thank you for your constant support.

To my friends, the survivors' group – Josh, Tim, Cal, Sammy, Rhiannon, Charlie, Paul, Olivia.

The list of people I want to thank is endless and I wouldn't be who I am today without all the support I have received over the years, all the young people I've worked with and the care community that I continue to work alongside. Thank you for your resilience and passion. Together, we will make a difference.

I would like to give a special thank you to my family. My mum, my sister Donna, my grandma, my cousin Andy Guy and the in-laws, Maria, Stella and Tony – thank you for everything that you do. Thank you to my son Bobby, my daughter Antonia and baby David, who is due to arrive on 5 July 2021. Last, but not least, thank you to my amazing wife Androulla. You are my rock and I love you so much. What a journey, we made it!

Finally, to my grandad, Eddie, who died of Covid in 2020. Sorry you're not going to see this book become a reality, but I know you will be looking down with pride. This one's for you. X

Chris Wild and Neil Morrissey,

in conversation

Chris: When I try and explain the care home I was in to people, it's the closest thing to a nightmare I can imagine. When I wrote my first book, *Damaged*, I went to investigate and find other people who I was in care with. That's what triggered how big of a scandal it was, because everybody who was in my room, four boys, all of them killed themselves before they were 21. Finding that out really hit home for me because I felt guilty for years. I felt guilty because I survived. I think about it to this day. I can't even imagine what kind of pain they went through.

The care sector hasn't changed in 30 years, but the world has. The NHS has changed, education has changed, but the care sector hasn't. There's still this massive stigma attached to being in care. You're always walking around tarnished.

Neil: Part of the problem is that we self-stigmatise, don't we? Once I got out of my care home I was in foster care for a while, which has still got a certain amount of stigma attached to it. I was lucky enough to get fostered from a care home to a nice family. Then, when I got to drama school, I became interesting because I'd been in a care home and people wanted to know what life was like in there.

My brother was in a place called Riverside, and it was a hotpot of abuse. I remember visiting, and they had to clean the whole foyer with a toothbrush. Stephen died young, he was about 26. He had a motorbike accident at about 20, and developed some kind of schizophrenia, but he wouldn't take his medication. He kept getting himself into trouble fighting. Everyone was scared of him. His life just went from bad to worse, getting in trouble, and he did a stretch in prison for stabbing someone. His behavior in prison was really bad, so he did the full six years. He came out, then after a couple of years, he was found dead in a flat in Wolverhampton. Everyone thinks he might have tried heroin for the first time. There were some puncture marks on his arm, and he was only recognisable by his tattoos.

We put him to rest by a place called Seven Springs, in a beautiful bit of countryside by these babbling brooks. We buried him there with a can of lager. We were all damaged in our own ways from being in care. There are good people out there, there are good foster homes, but in general, the system doesn't work, does it?

Chris: No. And it was built broken. I get a lot of young people saying to me, 'Why doesn't the system work? Why won't the system help me?' A lot of the young people I work with now, they'll make references to *Toy Story* and broken toys, 'Oh, that's a bit like me, isn't it, where I just get abandoned. Nobody wants me.' *The State of It* was important to me to write because I have to try and explain to a bigger audience that this is still happening, that the most vulnerable young people in our country, the ones who we should be supporting the most, the ones who we should be creating opportunities for, are just left in the dark. There's no support, and that's what I can't comprehend. They're human beings, Neil, and they've still got dreams and aspirations like me and you. But they don't have the same opportunities as their peers, and that's what I can't fathom. I can't grasp how we just can't look after these people, why we don't care about them.

Neil: We need to be empowering these people. It's about understanding what your worth is as a human in society.

Chris: And this is difficult. I still travel the country, go into organisations and speak to people, and hit a brick wall because you've got to try and sell a young person an education, you've got to try and sell a young person a better way of living. They turn around and say, 'Why?' They're reading the papers, they're watching the news. They know the economy is messed up.

When you do finally leave the care sector, you go into independent care at 16 and stay there til you're 18. Then, when you're 18, you go to panel. You're given an independent flat, a shared house in the middle of nowhere.

Neil: None of that was available when I was coming out of care.

Chris: But even then, at 18, you've got to get two or three jobs, maybe cleaning or any labouring jobs, to pay water and gas, as your peers who were living at home get the opportunity to go to university. If *you* want to go to university, you've got to work extra hard. I always say most people are born three-nil up. Care home kids are constantly trying to level up.

Neil: Yeah, that's right.

Chris: Only eight per cent of care leavers go on to further education. You are no longer a problem of the state. You are your own problem, and that's where you fall off the care cliff.

Neil: When I turned 17, they said, 'You can't carry on with

your education.' I was still at sixth form college but I had to go and get a job. So, they actively said, 'You are not going to have an education anymore.' That's when I put a notice up on the notice board saying, 'Foster parents urgently required.' I did find really good foster parents and stayed with them til I was 18 and got my A-levels. By that time, I was auditioning at drama school and managed to secure auditions in London.

I applied to the council because how am I going to get the money to get to London for the day to do an audition? I was very excited about it. The council refused, and I've still got that letter: 'We don't think this is a good option for Neil to be doing this kind of thing.' Hang on a minute, you should be praising kids for taking the initiative! Well, I did then get a Saturday job and got myself the money that you had to pay to go and audition, and for the return fair to London.

I got recalled, so I put another application in: '6,000 people have auditioned and 200 people are being called back,' so that's an achievement. 'No, no, no. You still don't qualify for any extra.'

Chris: How do you feel, now you've become successful, now you're doing well? Do you ever feel that you don't fit in with your peers? Do you ever feel like you are an outcast still?

Neil: I've always felt like I'm an interesting specimen to other actors. It's always a moment when I go, 'Yeah, I was brought up in care.' It's funny how, when you go through this business, you do find one or two people that were brought up in care, or spent a bit of time in foster care, but I think we're the very lucky few. I'm playing the outsider in roles. It's always been fine for me. I don't really have to do too much research.

I still feel like I self-stigmatise. Say me and my misses have a row about something, I just refuse to talk about it. I'll go away and have a think for a few days, maybe even a week, and then I'll be able to talk about it, 'Well, I did it because of this.' I think that's partly because, if there was ever a problem in my youth, you didn't say anything because a bunch of social workers would turn up, things would be written and your headmaster would be told, and then you'd have to go in and see them. And you're going, 'God, I just want to be fricking normal.' So, I just stopped saying things, stopped talking to people.

Drama school, or trauma school, as they call it, is about getting some of those emotions out in the open and exploring them. The whole of acting is about that. Whether you're writing or perform-ing, it's about exploring what comes out from inside you. I always tell other kids and people who experienced the care system that I use all of it as tools. That's my armory. I'm good at making a conversation because I had to meet new people all the time. I'm good at changing locations and all this kind of stuff because I'm a survivor and I can be by myself.

When I was 18, I could not wait to get away. I had a vision, since I was probably 13, to try to achieve normality. That was my main ambition.

I ended up being some mad leading actor, dressing up and speaking other people's words for a living.

Chris: I had to say to myself, 'You know what, Chris, you had a bad upbringing. This happened to you, but you can't let it destroy you.' My nightmares are all about: what if?

The only way you can make a difference is by talking about it.

I have endless meetings with MPs, with professionals who have been doing this for years, with people who have 20 degrees, but no one has a clue. I've been offered jobs to work backstage in politics, and I say no, because I'd be a hypocrite. My work, my duty of care, is to defend young people, and I'll do it until I die. I don't care about being a millionaire or making loads of money. I care about making a difference before I exit this world. I've lived for years with guilt, guilt because I survived. Now, to eradicate that guilt, I feel that I have a duty to help people.

When I go into an organisation I tell them, 'This is all wrong. Why are you just giving young people the opportunities to be a builder – let's broaden their horizon. Let's open the doors and give these young people a chance of life.' I'm currently doing a project with the London Ambulance crew, where we're getting young people work experience with them. I've got these young people saying, 'Oh, my God, I would never have got this opportunity.' No, you wouldn't, but these are the kind of opportunities you *should* be getting.

Neil: There's a friend of mine who makes films, and she gets prison leavers involved. Ninety per cent of them were brought up in care or foster homes, and all came from the care system.

Chris: That's how we're going to change it. We've got to start lifting and being more positive.

This is an edited transcript of a conversation between Chris Wild and Neil Morrissey. You can find the whole conversation at the end of the audiobook edition of The State of It, *available now from John Blake Publishing, an imprint of Bonnier Books UK.*